giving thanks

giving thanks

Thanksgiving Recipes and History, from Pilgrims to Pumpkin Pie

Kathleen Curtin,
Sandra L. Oliver, and
Plimoth Plantation

Clarkson Potter/Publishers
New York

Published in the United States by Clarkson Potter/
Publishers, an imprint of the Crown Publishing Group,
a division of Random House, Inc., New York.
www.crownpublishing.com
www.clarksonpotter.com

Clarkson N. Potter is a trademark and Potter
and colophon are registered trademarks of
Random House, Inc.

Library of Congress Cataloging-in-Publication Data
Giving thanks / the Plimoth Plantation—1st ed.
    1. Thanksgiving Day—History amd recipes.
2. Pilgrims (New Plymouth Colony)   3. Wampanoag
People—History—17th century.   4. New England—
Social life and customs—to 1775.   5. Thanksgiving Day.
6. United States—Social life and customs. I. Plimoth
Plantation, Inc.
F7.G585 2005
394.2649—dc22   2004024373

ISBN 1-4000-8057-6

Printed in Singapore

Design by Jennifer K. Beal

10 9 8 7 6 5 4 3 2 1

First Edition

frontispiece: Schools were used to teach children across the nation, both immigrant and native-born, about American traditions. *The Plymouth Scene,* Historic Pageant, Lowell School, Philadelphia, 1922.

Acknowledgments and Thanks

To the wonderful folks along the way who believed in this project and kept it alive-Lawrence Allen, Nancy Brennan (the chief cheerleader and godmother of *Giving Thanks*), Lisa deMauro, Ivan Lipton, Liz Lodge, Josh Mills and Jacques de Spoelberch.

To the creative team at Clarkson Potter: Pam Krauss, Christopher Pavone, Jennifer K. Beal, Felix Gregorio, and Mark McCauslin. Extra special thanks are due to the unflappable Adina Steiman for always being a calm, cheerful, and capable voice at the end of the phone line. Best of luck in your new endeavors.

To the many people who so generously shared their family's Thanksgiving recipes and traditions. While only a fraction of these recipes made their way onto these pages, all of your contributions helped us to better understand and represent Thanksgiving in these pages.

To the members of the Wampanoag Nation and other Native communities who came together at Plimoth Plantation in October 2000 to participate in the re-creation of the 1621 Harvest celebration. Several of the images taken over those three days grace this book. Particular thanks to Linda Coombs and Nancy Eldredge, who have helped us look at the past (and present) with fresh eyes.

To the many people and institutions who generously allowed us the use of their images or published recipes including: ACH Food (Karo Syrup), Anthony Dias Blue, Brady Enterprises (Bell's Seasoning) California Museum of Photography, University of California Riverside, The Cartoon Bank, Condé Nast, Curtis Publishing Company, Denver Public Library, HarperCollins, Library of Congress, Macy's East, Inc., Maine Historical Society, Mississippi Department of Archives and History, National Association of Congregational Christian Churches, Nestlé USA, Ed Nute, Ocean Spray Cranberries, Inc. (with special thanks to Christine Hormell) , *The Patriot Ledger*, Pilgrim Hall Museum, Random House, the Norman Rockwell Family Agency, Loren St. Onge, The Schlesinger Library, Radcliffe Institute, Harvard University, and the Harry S. Truman Library.

Last but by no means least, grateful thanks to Pat Baker, Karin Goldstein, Jill Hall, Marcia Hix, Maretta Mullen, Carolyn Travers, and Lisa Whalen. This book would not have been possible without your constant help, keen eyes for detail, and unflagging encouragement.

Contents

PART II

The Recipes

THANKSGIVING — DAY.

THE UNION ALTAR.

Introduction

If there is one day each year when food and family
take center stage, it is Thanksgiving. It is a holiday about "going home"—with all the emo-
tional content those two words imply. The Sunday following Thanksgiving is always the
busiest travel day of the year in the United States. Each day of the long Thanksgiving
weekend, more than 10 million people take to the skies. Another 40 million Americans
drive 100 miles or more to have Thanksgiving dinner. And the nation's railways teem with
travelers going home for the holiday. Despite modern-day turmoil and change—in many
cases, because of it—the lure of a Thanksgiving celebration with friends and family proves
irresistible to Americans.

At its heart, Thanksgiving is about comfort, ritual, and nostalgia for a simpler time. In a
nation of restaurant-goers and fast-food consumers, nine out of ten Americans sit down to
a *home-cooked* holiday feast featuring turkey, gravy, stuffing (or dressing, if you hail from the
South), and an ever-growing number of side dishes, pies, and desserts. Thanksgiving is the
quintessential American holiday. Americans of many faiths and ethnic backgrounds celebrate Thanksgiving in every corner of the country. They visit friends and family and remi-
nisce about everything from memorable holiday cooking disasters to loved ones who are no
longer at the table. They watch parades and football. They cook both traditional and untra-
ditional Thanksgiving dishes and sample unique family recipes that are often rolled out just
for the holiday. They set a bountiful table and share a meal in concert with the whole nation.

Thanksgiving naturally brings to mind the oft-told story of "The First Thanksgiving."
Each fall, images abound of the Pilgrims and the native Wampanoag—the unwitting
founders of this American tradition. While the story may seem to date from the arrival of
the *Mayflower*, the historic events of "The First Thanksgiving" were unknown to most
Americans until hundreds of years later. The evolution of the Thanksgiving holiday and its
cuisine is a great deal more complex than the simple, mythic tale Americans learn as children. The history of the holiday involves not only the native Wampanoag People and the
English who settled at Plymouth but also the Civil War, a half-dozen presidents, one *very*
persistent woman, innovations in food and food technology, immigrants from all over the
world, and an evolving sense of what it is to be an American.

left: Thanksgiving was politicized during the divisive Civil War. *Thanksgiving Day*, by Thomas Nast, from
Harper's Weekly, December 5, 1863.

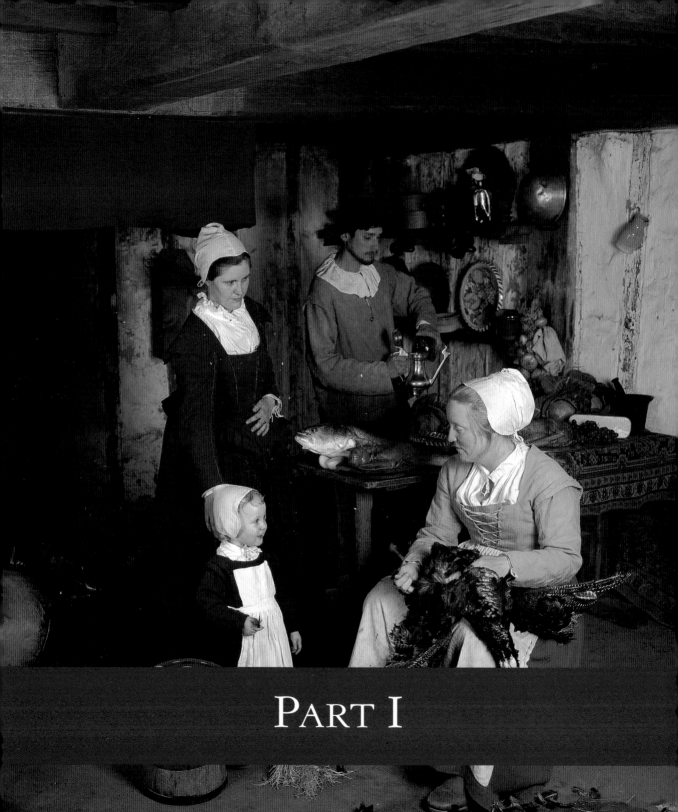

PART I

Thanksgiving
Then and Now

1621:
The First Thanksgiving?

Every American is familiar with the traditional Thanksgiving meal—roast turkey with stuffing, cranberry sauce, sweet potatoes, and, of course, pumpkin pie. As we eat these classic dishes year after year, we have a sense of continuing a tradition that began with the "Pilgrims and Indians." But are these really the foods the English colonists and native Wampanoag ate together during the harvest celebration in 1621, the event that has come to be known as "The First Thanksgiving"?

The images and particulars of this long-ago autumn celebration are so familiar that many people mistakenly believe that the event and the food were thoroughly documented. Would that this were true! Unfortunately, the only written record of the celebration mentions just two food items—deer and wildfowl—and doesn't give a hint about what else was eaten or how the food was prepared or served. For that information, we need to look to other seventeenth-century sources—European paintings and drawings, period cookbooks, artifacts, Wampanoag oral histories, archaeological evidence, and the journals and writings of the colonists themselves—to make educated guesses about details of the celebration.

There may have been turkey; wild turkeys were plentiful in New England, and both the native Wampanoag and the English colonists ate them. A small turkey may even have been roasted—on a spit in front of a fire, not in the oven, as today. The roast turkey could have been stuffed with onions, chestnuts, or garden herbs. There may have been cranberries during the three days of feasting, as they were available in the wild. But the sweetened condiment we now call cranberry sauce was not yet part of the English cooking tradition, even if the colonists had had the sugar needed to sweeten the tart berries. The sweet potato was not known to the Wampanoag at the time, and though it was eaten in England by 1620, it was not grown in the colonial gardens of Plymouth. There were no mashed white potatoes either, for that matter, as this type of potato was unknown to both the Wampanoag and the English. And what about pumpkin pie, the favorite Thanksgiving dessert? Unlikely. There were pumpkins and squashes,

preceding page: Plimoth Plantation re-creation of a colonial woman plucking a turkey. Clams, lobster, and fish can also be seen in the picture. *left:* The full painting depicts the actual number of colonists and Wampanoag People mentioned in Edward Winslow's letter. Detail, *The First Thanksgiving, 1621,* by Karen Rinaldo, 1995.

or *pompions,* as the English called them, but recipes for pumpkin pie don't appear until a bit later in the century, and the ovens needed to bake pies were not a likely part of the colony at this early point in its history.

Clearly, many of the traditional dishes of our Thanksgiving dinner were not present at the 1621 celebration. Ironically, when trying to discover what *was* on the menu, it is often easier to make judgments about what was probably not there. Figuring out just what was served—and what the three-day harvest celebration was *really* like—is a much tougher nut to crack.

 WAMPANOAG TRADITIONS OF GIVING THANKS

By Nancy Eldredge, Educator and Nauset Wampanoag

The American custom of thanksgiving did not begin with the arrival of the European colonists. Giving thanks for the Creator's gifts is an integral part of Wampanoag daily life. From ancient times up to the present, Native People of North America have held ceremonies to give thanks for successful harvests, for the hope of a good growing season in the early spring, and for other good fortune such as the birth of a child. Giving thanks was the primary reason for ceremonies or celebrations.

During the sixteenth and seventeenth centuries, Europeans came to our homeland. They commented in their writings about all the wonderful foods that were found in nature, and the richness and abundance of berries, wild grapes, fish and shellfish, deer, wild turkey, and more. The people indigenous to this area were well aware of this abundance. For generations and generations, the Wampanoag knew of certain times and seasons to collect the berries, and medicines from plants, when to hunt and fish, and how to ensure that there would be food for the future generations of their people. One of those ways was in the daily giving of thanks for the abundance of materials that were given from the Creator for everyday life. By keeping gratefulness in mind, the Creator's gifts were not taken for granted. Thankfulness was woven into every aspect of Wampanoag life. If an animal was hunted for food, special thanks were given to the Creator and to the spirit of the animal. If a plant was harvested and used for any purpose, if a bird or fish was taken, even if an anthill was disrupted, acknowledgment and gratitude were given for the lives that were taken. To this day it is the same with most Native People.

A single eyewitness account of the 1621 harvest celebration survives, buried in a letter written in December of that year by colonist Edward Winslow to a friend in England:

Our harvest being gotten in, our governor sent four men on fowling, that so we might after a special manner rejoice together after we had gathered the fruit of our labors. They four in one day killed as much fowl as, with a little help beside, served the company almost a week. At which time, amongst other recreations, we exercised our arms, many of the Indians coming amongst us, and among the rest their great king Massasoit, with some ninety men, whom for three days we entertained and feasted, and they went out and killed five deer, which they brought to the plantation and bestowed on our governor, and upon the captain and others. And although it be not always so plentiful as it was at this time with us, yet by the goodness of God, we are so far from want that we often wish you partakers of our plenty.

"Partakers of Our Plenty"

So what *do* we know? The harvest celebration of 1621 occurred sometime between September 21 and November 9, the time of year that the native Wampanoag People called *Keepunumuk,* the time of harvest. The event lasted at least three days and took place in the town the English called Plymouth, known to the Native People as Patuxet. This town was in the middle of the Wampanoag homeland.

In a bountiful seventeenth-century New England, the autumn months were particularly generous. The harvest of native, or Indian, corn, the primary crop of the Wampanoag and then the colonists, coincided with the return of migratory geese and ducks to the area. For the colonists at Plymouth, who had come through a very difficult first year, the modest success of their first harvest and the abundance of the fall season were reason to celebrate in a traditional English manner. So William Bradford, the governor of Plymouth Plantation, sent four men out to hunt for wildfowl for a harvest celebration. At some point during the celebration, Massasoit, an important *sachem* (leader) of the Wampanoag People, along with ninety Native men and an unknown number of other Native People, joined the English for three days of entertainment, feasting, and diplomacy.

Harvest Home or Thanksgiving?

To the English of Plymouth Plantation, what is now referred to as "The First Thanksgiving" was neither a first nor a thanksgiving. The three days of feasting, diplomacy, and recreation were a harvest feast or harvest "home"—a traditional celebration in many agricultural societies. In England, a successful harvest marked the end of the year's labor and the beginning of the "fat" time of the year, when good food was more abundant and the work was often less strenuous. On larger holdings, the celebrations were elaborate, with everyone in the neighborhood invited to a day of feasting and entertainment. Even small-scale farmers provided a harvest supper at the end of the year's agricultural labor.

Thanksgiving, on the other hand, had a precise and special meaning to the English—it was a solemn day of prayer and worship to thank God for a special providence (blessing). Special national days of thanksgiving, declared by the English government in response to specific events, were an important part of English life. Some of these thanksgivings recognized one-time-only events, such as the safe return of the royal heir from abroad. Annual thanksgivings were also held to commemorate important events. A well-known example is Guy Fawkes Day, known in the seventeenth century as (Gun) Powder Treason Day. On November 5, 1605, a small band of assassins led by Guy Fawkes plotted to blow up Parliament during the King's visit. The conspiracy was discovered, and the men were apprehended. The nation celebrated the event's anniversary with religious services, bonfires, and feasts.

English Puritans made thanksgiving a day of purely religious worship as part of their attempt to reform the Christian calendar. Instead of the traditional holidays, Christmas and Easter, Puritans observed three holy-days, or holidays: the Sabbath, Days of Thanksgiving and Praise, and Days of Fasting and Humiliation. Disliking annual commemorations, Puritans declared thanksgiving days in response to specific instances of divine favor. Many of these same English Puritans colonized Plymouth and, a bit later, much of New England, bringing their practices and beliefs with them. The English at Plymouth recorded their first thanksgiving in 1623. This solemn gathering was in response to the end of a drought, and there is no mention of food or a feast in connection with it.

Let Them Eat . . . Meat!

For years, Americans assumed a direct connection between their Thanksgiving holiday menu of turkey, pumpkin pie, and mashed potatoes and the 1621 harvest celebration. In truth, there is no exact record of the bill of fare for the 1621 celebration, and many beloved Thanksgiving foods, including mashed potatoes and apple pie, were simply impossible in 1621. For those searching for a deeper symbolism in their turkey, the strongest connection between the 1621 harvest celebration and the later Thanksgiving holiday menu is that both were based on foods with New England roots.

According to the only eyewitness account of the 1621 harvest celebration (see page 15), venison was a principal food on the menu. The presence of venison was significant for several reasons, one of them being the simple fact that people of both cultures liked to eat it. But venison was more to the two cultures than just a favorite food. In England, venison was rarely part of the common man's experience. Deer were found only in the parks and forests of the landed gentry. Venison was not commercially available (by *law,* you could not buy or sell it), and it is likely that few, if any, of the colonists had eaten it before coming to New England. Venison was a meat that had real status—a true class marker. In contrast, deer was central to the Wampanoag way of life, providing tools,

clothes, and food. The Wampanoag gift and ceremonial presentation of five deer to the chief Englishmen was essential to the diplomacy taking place over the course of the harvest celebration. The exchange of gifts was (and still is) common among the Wampanoag to show respect and friendship.

opposite: Harvest celebrations were part of the colonists' European heritage. This scene shows harvest in the month of August in the Netherlands. *Augustus,* an engraving from *The Twelve Months* by Jan van de Velde, 1616. *above*: Plimoth Plantation re-creation of Wampanoag men hunting deer.

The Wampanoag are a Native nation composed of a number of individual tribes. *Wampanoag* means "Eastern People" or "People of the First Light." The Wampanoag homeland includes the territory along the East Coast from Wessagusset (today called Weymouth, Massachusetts) to what is now Cape Cod and the islands of Natocket and Noepe (now called Nantucket and Martha's Vineyard), southeast as far as Pokanocket (now called Bristol and Warren, Rhode Island), and to the northeast corner of present-day Rhode Island.

Wildfowl (as opposed to domestic barnyard fowl), another favorite celebratory food, were also plentiful during the celebration. To prepare for the 1621 feast, English hunters brought back enough wildfowl to feed the "company [the group or the village] for almost a week," as noted by Edward Winslow, a Plymouth colonist and sole chronicler of the 1621 event. Given his description of the hunt and the number of birds the hunters brought in, it is likely that Winslow's "fowl" were the thousands of ducks and geese that made their way to the area each fall. Several journals and letters of the colonists, including this one from John Pory, a 1623 visitor to Plymouth, describe the astounding seasonal abundance of waterfowl: "From the beginning of September till the end of March, their bay in a manner is covered with all sorts of water fowl, in such sort of swarms and multitudes as is rather admirable than credible." It is also possible that smaller wood birds such as ruffed grouse, bobwhites (American quail), and the now extinct heath hens and passenger pigeons were present during the many meals that celebrated that harvest, since the birds were abundant in New England at the time and were eaten by both cultures. English traveler William Wood described the amazing flocks of passenger pigeons he saw in New England in 1634: "I have seen them fly as if the airy regiment had been pigeons, seeing neither beginning nor ending, length or breadth of these millions and millions. The shouting of people, the rattling of guns, and pelting of small shot could not drive them out of their course, but so continued for four or five hours together."

And what about turkey? It is very probable that turkey was on the table. There were many wild turkeys in and around the forests of Plymouth. (Sadly, by the 1640s, the population of turkeys had been decimated by overhunting.) William Wood described the New England turkey as "a very large bird, of a black color yet white in flesh, much bigger than our English turkey. He hath the use of his long legs so ready that he can run as fast as a dog and fly as well as a goose. Of these sometimes there will be forty, threescore, and an hundred of a flock, sometimes more and sometimes less."

Turkeys, while native to North America, were already a familiar sight to the English; turkeys had been taken to England by way of Spain by the mid-1500s and had become an instant hit as a celebratory food, particularly on the Christmas table.

Fish and Shellfish

All year round, New England's sea, shore, and rivers were a bountiful resource to the English colonists and native Wampanoag People. While the summertime abundance of bluefish, bass, and cod no longer ran in the bay nearby, mussels, lobsters, eels, and other fish were available in the fall. Fish and shellfish were considered a "lesser meat" than fowl or red meat such as venison, but the need to provide a variety of foods to a large number of diners over the course of three days may have meant that fish and shellfish made their way to the tables. Both the English and the Wampanoag enjoyed eating eels; John Pory wrote in 1623 that he found the eels in Plymouth to be "passing sweet, fat and wholesome, having no taste at all of the mud, and are as great as ever I saw any." Mussels, clams, and lobsters were easily harvested on the shores. Pory reported that the lobsters he saw were "so large, so full of meat, and so plentiful in number as no man will believe that hath not seen. For a knife of three halfpence, I bought ten lobsters that would well have dined forty labouring men."

Native Corn

The 1621 celebration was held after the harvest of the colorful hard flint corn, or maize, that the English often referred to as *Indian corn*. In early accounts, the English used this new term to distinguish it from English "corns" like wheat, rye, and barley. This corn was a staple for the Wampanoag and soon became a fixture in the cooking pots of Plymouth. The English acquired their first seed corn by helping themselves to a cache from a Native storage pit during one of their initial explorations of Cape Cod. (They later paid the Native owners for this "borrowed" corn.) It is likely that the English colonists processed and prepared the novel corn for the first time in the fall of 1621. The colonists sought to describe and prepare this new grain in famil-

above: Plimoth Plantation re-creation of Wampanoag women gathering mussels along the coast.

iar, comforting terms: "Our Indian corn, even the coarsest, maketh as pleasant a meat as rice," wrote Edward Winslow in 1621. Colonial housewives used the new corn in traditional English ways—as a porridge, pudding, or thickener in meat stews.

Fruits and Vegetables

Both cultivated and wild fruits and vegetables were available in September and October, though they were probably not eaten with the same degree of pleasure as the meat and corn dishes. The English had a complex relationship with vegetables. To many of them, vegetables were a secondary and inferior food, though throughout the 1600s the upper classes (and anyone who aspired to be like them) began to add more fruits and vegetables to their diet, both in quantity and variety. The early autumn produce from the gardens of Plymouth probably included cabbages, carrots, cucumbers, coleworts (collards), endive, fennel, green beet (chard), leeks, lettuce, marjoram, mint, onions, parsnips, parsley, pompions (pumpkins), radish, spinach, sage, winter savory, thyme, turnips, and violet leaves. Native wild plants known and used by the Wampanoag, including Jerusalem artichokes, wild onions, garlic, and watercress, were available in the fall. Most native fruits were out of season, but cranberries and Concord grapes were available in the early autumn, as were a number of native nuts, including walnuts and chestnuts.

"Stirring Up the Pot"

We don't know exactly what foodstuffs were carried aboard the *Mayflower,* or how much of that supply was still left by the autumn of 1621, but other ships to New England were known to bring in a variety of spices, seasonings, and other items. Even in small amounts, imports such as wine, dried fruits (currants, prunes, raisins), pepper, sugar, ginger, nutmeg, cinnamon, and mustard would have gone a long way toward helping to "stir up the pot" and adding a pleasing and familiar taste to foods. There is a good chance that eggs and goat milk were available from the English domestic animals as well. (While there is no record of farm animals aboard the *Mayflower,* later accounts of the colony suggest that chickens, pigs, and goats did in fact come across on the first voyage.)

above: A Wampanoag woman grinds corn with a mortar and pestle, a method adopted by the English before they built a mill.

And to Wash It Down . . .

It is probable—and presumably regrettable, from the colonists' viewpoint—that the beverage served and drunk during those days of celebration was simple water. Although a number of English accounts refer favorably to the wonderful "sweet" qualities of New England's water, there can be no doubt that beer was greatly missed. In England, beer was the ordinary daily drink consumed by everyone regardless of age, gender, or class. It was also consumed in quantities that are quite frankly staggering to a modern person. (For instance, a frequent shipboard ration was a gallon a day per man.) In their first year, the English colonists grew a few acres of barley, so it is possible that some beer or ale was brewed by the end of harvest time—but, given how long it takes to brew and ferment beer, this seems unlikely. Wine, considered a finer beverage than beer, may have been brought across the Atlantic by some travelers on the *Mayflower;* it was frequently mentioned in later accounts of supplies to the colonies. By the mid-1600s, cider had become the main beverage of New Englanders, but in 1621 Plymouth did not yet have apples, except for the native crab apple, which was not used for cider.

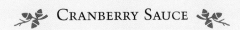

CRANBERRY SAUCE

The first descriptions of cranberry sauce and cranberry tarts were written more than fifty years after the arrival of the *Mayflower.* In both of these dishes, the sour cranberries are sweetened with a good deal of sugar—which probably was not available in any great quantity at Plymouth in 1621. It is possible, however, that an English housewife used cranberries unsweetened in her cookery. It was customary in English cookery of that time to use tart berries or grapes to sharpen broths and sauces. In 1643, Roger Williams, a colonial minister, provided the earliest written description of the fruit: "a kind of sharp Fruit like a Barbary [the sour red fruit of the barberry bush] in taste." He doesn't call them *cranberries* but rather gives the name used by the native Narragansett People, *sasemineash.*

Of Cooks and Cookery

Preparing for the large and lengthy feast event for fifty colonists and more than one hundred Native People was undoubtedly an enormous undertaking for the colony. One long-held and popular story of the 1621 celebration was that the four surviving English housewives did all the cooking, but this seems very unlikely. It is true that after the sickness of the first winter, only four married women remained of the twenty wives who came on the *Mayflower*. However, numerous children, servants, and unmarried men (and probably more than a few married ones) were no doubt marshaled to provide the labor needed for such a celebration.

What we know about English cooking leads us to believe that over the course of the feasting a combination of roasted and boiled dishes were served. Pieces of venison and whole wildfowl were placed on spits and roasted before glowing coals while other cooking took place in the household hearths. It is easy to speculate that large brass pots for cooking corn, meat pottages (stews), or simple boiled vegetables ("sallets") were in constant use. The meaty carcasses from one meal no doubt were simmered to yield broth for use in the next. In the English tradition, the meats may have had accompanying sauces—perhaps something as simple as mustard, a popular English "sauce." Contrary to conventional wisdom, the seventeenth-century English cookery revealed through cookbooks of the time was anything but bland, making skillful use of spices, herbs, dried fruits, wine, and beer.

🌺 "So Where Are the Pilgrims?" 🌺

You may have noticed that the word *pilgrim* is not used in this chapter to describe the colonists of Plymouth. The term was used rarely in the surviving writings of the early colonists. More than twenty years after the arrival of the *Mayflower*, William Bradford, the governor of the colony, wrote about his exiled church's departure from Leiden, Holland, to America. Referring to Scripture, as he often did, he wrote, "[T]hey knew they were pilgrims." Then, as now, the word pilgrim meant someone on a journey with a religious or moral purpose.

Bradford did not use *pilgrim* as a label or title for the English in Plymouth Colony. Around 1800, this quotation was taken out of context by historians and theologians and applied to everyone in Plymouth Colony, including those who were not part of the Leiden congregation Bradford described. The name gained popularity and remains in common usage today to describe all of the early Plymouth colonists.

Was Wampanoag Food Served?

Clearly, almost everything that was eaten at the harvest feasts consisted of the indigenous foods of the Wampanoag homeland. Whether traditional Wampanoag dishes were served at the 1621 celebration hinges on the question of whether or not Native women were there. While Native women are not mentioned specifically in the eyewitness account, a careful reading of Edward Winslow's letter combined with cultural information from Wampanoag historians leaves open the possibility that Wampanoag women may indeed have participated in the event. The relevant passage reads, "many of the Indians coming amongst us, and among the rest their great king Massasoit, with some ninety men." Clearly, in addition to Massasoit and his ninety men there were other Native People. Those present probably included local Wampanoag families, such as the family of Hobbamock, a Native *pniese* (warrior-counselor) who lived alongside the English. Hobbamock had a household of ten people, including several wives who could have attended. Wampanoag historians also believe that Massasoit may have traveled with one or more of his wives.

Dining and Feasting

Traditional nineteenth- and twentieth-century images of the so-called First Thanksgiving display a single feast with everyone gathered around a groaning banquet table. It is *possible* that the celebration was like that, but not *likely*. The written description from 1621 tells us that Massasoit and his men were entertained for three days. The whole celebration may indeed have been longer. Over those several days, many meals would have been offered and eaten. What we know about the celebration and English and Wampanoag eating and social customs makes other dining scenarios more likely than the single great table of popular imagination.

Vast cultural differences and an atmosphere of wariness undoubtedly existed between the Wampanoag and the English. The harvest celebration was a meeting of divergent groups who did not speak the same language or understand the world in the same way. In general, the seventeenth-century English, including the colonists at Plymouth, were suspicious of anyone who was not English. In their writings, leading colonists are critical of the customs, household arrangements, and, most especially, the religion of the Wampanoag. The Wampanoag had already learned to be wary of Europeans, who brought disease and guns and kidnapped Native

above: The whole village most likely helped prepare meals for the harvest celebration. A young man is turning a spit to roast a goose in this Plimoth Plantation re-creation.

❧ WAMPANOAG AUTUMN SOBAHEG ❧

Sobaheg is the Wampanoag word for "stew." Like most stews, this dish is easily adapted to seasonal ingredients. This version is suitable for harvest time and is made with venison, but the recipe lends itself beautifully to other types of meat. Try it with turkey, goose, duck, fish, or shellfish. Variations of this dish are still made in Wampanoag households in New England. Like other cuisines, Wampanoag cookery has continued to evolve, incorporating new ingredients and techniques with the traditional.

Salt is not mentioned in the original recipe, even though it was probably used when the recipe was recorded in 1674. Before trade with Europeans, the Wampanoag got the salt necessary for good health by consuming seafood. After the arrival of the English, salt became a popular trade commodity with the Wampanoag. This Wampanoag recipe appears here instead of in the main recipe section to respect the perspective of the many Wampanoag and other Native People who choose not to celebrate the American Thanksgiving holiday.

Their food is generally boiled maize or Indian corn, mixed with kidney-beans, or sometimes without. Also they frequently boil in this pottage fish and flesh of all sorts, either taken fresh or newly dried. These they cut in pieces, bones and all, and boil them in the aforesaid pottage. I have wondered many times that they were not in danger of being choked with fish bones; but they are so dexterous to separate the bones from the fish in the eating thereof, that they are in no hazard. Also they boil in this furmenty all sorts of flesh, that they take in hunting; as venison, beaver, bear's flesh, moose, otters, rackoons, or any kind that they take in hunting; cutting this flesh in small pieces, and boiling as aforesaid. Also they mix with the said pottage several sorts of roots; as Jerusalem artichokes, and ground nuts, and other roots, and pompions, and squashes, and also several sorts of nuts or masts, as oak acorns, chestnuts, walnuts; these husked and dried, and powdered, they thicken their pottage therewith.

—DANIEL GOOKINS, *HISTORICAL COLLECTIONS OF THE INDIANS IN NEW ENGLAND,* 1674.

Wampanoag Autumn Sobaheg: Modern Version

SERVES 6

½ cup dried beans
½ cup coarse grits (see sidebar, page 123)
1 pound venison or other meat, cut into bite-sized pieces
1 teaspoon salt
1 small acorn squash or 2 cups any other winter squash, peeled and cut into bite-sized pieces
1 cup peeled and cubed Jerusalem artichokes (see Note)
¼ cup walnuts, chestnuts, or sunflower seeds, shelled and ground until powdery

Combine the dried beans, grits, venison, salt, and 8 cups water in a large, heavy-bottomed pot. Bring the mixture to a gentle boil over medium heat. Cover the pot, reduce the heat, and keep the sobaheg at a low simmer. Cook approximately 2 hours, until the beans and venison are tender, stirring often to prevent sticking. Periodically skim off the froth that rises to the top. Stir in the squash and Jerusalem artichokes and simmer until they are done, about 30 minutes.

Add the nut flour, stirring until thoroughly blended, and serve.

NOTE: Jerusalem artichokes, also called *sunchokes*, are part of the sunflower family. They are available in market produce sections in the fall and early winter. If you are unable to find them, the recipe will still be delicious.

People. By the harvest of 1621, a number of awkward encounters and incidents had already shown the great lack of understanding between the two cultures. Colonists from Plymouth had appropriated corn that belonged to a Native family, investigated Wampanoag graves, and taken "some of the prettiest things" from a Wampanoag house. But there had been positive encounters as well. Some of the Wampanoag leaders, including Massasoit, made a strategic alliance with the colonists at Plymouth, and there had been occasional visits between the two peoples. All of these encounters and perspectives would have certainly influenced the dynamics of the

1621 celebration. Indeed, perhaps the cultural barriers were so wide that, aside from the most important men, the two populations were reserved, preferring to keep more familiar company. Even today, people thrown together in an unfamiliar social setting tend to stick to their own comfortable groups. But is this a phenomenon that crosses centuries? We will never know for sure, but based on what had already occurred between the two cultures, we can assume there was a range of interactions, from friendliness to cautious curiosity to real wariness.

Perhaps the important men, such as the sachem, Massasoit, and the colonial governor, William Bradford, feasted together, formally attended by a couple of servants. A meal of this sort may have been just as much about diplomacy as about dining, and in both English and Wampanoag cultures such gatherings were used to forge or cement strategic bonds. Seventeenth-century images and descriptions of each culture also suggest more casual dining arrangements with a number of activities happening at once. In England, weddings and other celebrations provided the centerpiece for a community celebration that could last for several days. In paintings depicting this type of community event, some people are dining while others are serving food, cooking, or at play. Throughout the year, the Wampanoag held casual feasts that lasted for days or even weeks. A colonial writer recorded that large numbers of Native People met together to feast "at a place where Lobsters come in with the tyde, to eat, and save dried for store, abiding in that place, feasting and sporting, a moneth or 6. weekes together." We may never know how the 1621 event played out over the several days, but the reality was certainly more complex than a single feast.

❧ "LOOK, MA, NO FORK!" ❧

There was not a single eating fork to be found in Plymouth in 1621. Both the English and the Wampanoag People ate with knives, spoons, and fingers. Knives were used both to cut food and to convey "gobbets" or morsels to the mouth.

In early seventeenth-century England, a variety of forks were in use, from those that held joints of meat for cutting to pitchforks used in farming. Eating forks were used at court, though to common Englishmen they smacked of a disdainful "foreignness." According to archaeologist James Deetz, forks were not common in England until the mid-1600s at the earliest. In New England, no eating forks have been found on any archaeological sites predating the early 1700s, and significant numbers don't appear until a few decades later.

above: A Plimoth Plantation re-creation of a scene from the 1621 harvest celebration, Wampanoag and Plymouth Colony leaders share a formal meal.

Irreconcilable Differences

The 1621 celebration shared by the English and Wampanoag is the only harvest feast in early Plymouth that we know about, and this event did not begin an annual tradition. Whatever friendly relations existed in the 1620s between the Wampanoag and the English colonists did not last long. Over the next few decades, the differences between them reached a crisis. In 1629, the Massachusetts Bay Colony was established, and English colonists began to pour into the area around Boston by the thousands. The increase in numbers led to rising tensions between the Native People and the colonists, and each year saw a worsening of relations. In 1636, war broke out between the English and the Pequot People who lived on the Connecticut River. That same year, Massachusetts Bay Colony governor John Winthrop proclaimed a day of thanksgiving to celebrate the defeat of their enemies, the Pequot. Though this was the first time that a day of thanksgiving was called to celebrate a victory over the Native People, it would not be the last. Finally, in 1675, a devastating conflict later called King Philip's War broke out between the English and the Wampanoag. In percentage terms, the war cost more lives and property damage than any other fought on American soil. The surviving Wampanoag lost much of their lands and their political independence. Wampanoag children were forced to be servants in English households, and Wampanoag captives were sold into slavery and sent to other colonies. This destructive pattern would be repeated time and time again as Europeans spread across the continent.

above: A Wampanoag hunter carries a turkey in this Plimoth Plantation re-creation. Turkeys were plentiful in the Wampanoag homeland in 1621, and were probably served at the 1621 harvest celebration.

From New England Tradition to National Holiday

By the end of the seventeenth century, days of thanksgiving had begun their evolution from austere, religious, church-based holy days to holidays that focused on family and food. In the New England colonies, it became usual to proclaim a day of thanksgiving in the autumn in addition to any other thanksgivings that were called for in the course of the year. The harvest celebration with the Wampanoag in the fall of 1621, as far as we know, was forgotten and played no part in the thanksgivings of the seventeenth and eighteenth centuries. There is not a single reference to the celebration until nearly 200 years later, when Alexander Young "discovered" and published Edward Winslow's 1621 letter.

Thanksgiving Evolves

The earliest colonial thanksgivings in the 1600s were sporadic and solemn religious and civil observances in recognition of specific blessings like a timely rainfall or peace after war, or as a more general expression of gratitude for prosperity and health. People spent the day attending morning and afternoon church services, and though they socialized between and after services, there was little time for a large meal. These general thanksgivings increasingly occurred in the fall and counterbalanced the annual spring Fast Days, which like thanksgivings were spent in church, with the faithful eating no food until late in the day.

Over the 1700s, thanksgiving observances evolved into a single autumn New England holiday centered on the family and a bountiful table, so that by the 1780s the outlines of the modern holiday were clear. By that time, the holiday had acquired many of the characteristics we are familiar with today. The old custom of two church services a day on Thanksgiving, as on Sunday, had loosened somewhat, which allowed for the dinner meal to expand into more than a bite between services. Nevertheless, worship was as much a cornerstone of late eighteenth-century Thanksgivings as family and dinner.

❧ CREATING THE FIRST THANKSGIVING ❧

In 1841, Alexander Young published his book, *Chronicles of the Pilgrim Forefathers.* One entry was the previously lost account in a letter by Edward Winslow of the events of 1621, written in December to a friend in England. In a footnote, Young named the harvest event Winslow described "The First Thanksgiving." Young even speculated about the probable menu that day, interpreting Winslow's mention of "fowl" as wild turkey, a perfectly natural thing for a New Englander of the 1840s to assume.

Young's footnote is the earliest named reference historians have found to the first Thanksgiving by name, but as the nineteenth century progressed, the phrase *First Thanksgiving* and the word *Pilgrim* became increasingly conflated with the celebration Winslow described, even though there is no indication whatsoever that the Plymouth colonists in attendance regarded the event as a thanksgiving, or even as their first thanksgiving.

Menu of the Day

As attitudes toward Thanksgiving changed from the 1600s to the 1800s, so did the food on the table. Upon first arriving in New England, English colonists prepared essentially English food, but within a generation, a cuisine emerged with distinctly American traits. In 1796, the first recorded recipes for several traditional Thanksgiving favorites appeared in the earliest American cookbook, *American Cookery,* by Amelia Simmons. Though Miss Simmons never specifies that the recipes are for the holiday, she describes "How to stuff a Turkey" and roast it and how to make a chicken pie, apple pie, "Pumpkin Pie," and "Minced Pies"—all Thanksgiving favorites of the era.

The pioneering American surgeon Mason Fitch Cogswell, born in 1761 in Canterbury, Connecticut, described a typical eighteenth-century Thanksgiving meal in his 1788 journal. He traveled to his native state from New York to spend Thanksgiving week with his father. Cogswell arrived the Saturday before the actual holiday, and in the following days, when the weather permitted, he visited with old friends, drank flip (a heated mixture of beer, liquor, and sugar) with them, and ate a little pre-Thanksgiving pumpkin pie. On Thanksgiving Day itself, he attended church in the morning, ate a dinner afterward consisting of turkey, pork, pumpkins, and apple pies, *and,* as he wrote, "etc., etc." Cogswell spent time with his father, then sang songs and ate apples and nuts in the kitchen with his stepsisters before going to bed. By 1845, Thanksgiving meals had become much more elaborate. Mrs. E. A. Howland, of Worcester, Massachusetts, describes a full Thanksgiving dinner in the back of her cookbook. Her menu specified roast turkey, stuffed; a pair of chickens stuffed and boiled with cabbage and a lean piece of pork; and a chicken pie. The vegetable side dishes included potatoes, turnips, squash, and onions boiled in milk. Both gravy *and* a gravy sauce with giblets, an applesauce, a cranberry sauce, and an oyster sauce accompanied the meat. White and brown bread were included. Plum and plain puddings, both with sweet sauce; mince, pumpkin, and apple pies; and cheese rounded out the meal. Similar menus appear in the contented recollections of people who grew up in this era. A resident of Great Falls, New Hampshire, Mary Channing, recalled around 1835, "A turkey was the principle dish; then there were chicken-pies, and vegetables, sauces, pickles, preserves; pie of mince, apple, squash, pumpkin, and custard; nuts, apples, raisins." In North Stonington, Connecticut, local historian Grace Denison Wheeler remembered Thanksgiving at her grandmother's house around 1869, which included "besides the turkey" chicken pies, roast pork, brown bread, cucumber pickles, pickled pears, mince, apple, and pumpkin pies, and homemade cheese, both plain and flavored with sage. Harriet Beecher Stowe's account in *Oldtown Folks* rings true: "But who shall . . . describe the turkey, and chickens, and chicken pies, with all that endless variety of vegetables which the American soil and climate have contributed to the table. . . . After the meat came the plum-puddings, and then the endless array of pies . . . [until] even we children turned from the profusion offered to us, and wondered what was the matter with us that we could eat no more."

This basic menu hardly changed through most of the 1800s, but by the end of the nineteenth century, there were some Victorian refinements. More genteel manners and table settings and a desire for more elegant fare had been trickling down for four hundred years from the nobility of the Renaissance and reached the American middle class in the mid-1800s. This desire, combined with cheaper and more plentiful manufactured ceramics, tableware, and linens, led to a grand Thanksgiving tablesetting with matching individual place settings, napkins, celery glasses (see page 32), castor sets to hold condiments, serving platters, and bowls, each with its own special purpose. Prosperous farmers and town-dwellers alike took their cues from publications like *Godey's Lady's Magazine* (edited by the same Sarah Josepha Hale who urged President Lincoln to declare Thanksgiving a national holiday). Middle-class homemakers attained a degree of elegance that a hundred years earlier only a handful of the gentry cared about.

Fannie Farmer's 1896 *Boston Cooking-School Cookbook* reflected this new refinement, offering a newly sophisticated Thanksgiving menu. Indulgent recipes included oyster soup with crackers, salted almonds, roast turkey, cranberry jelly, mashed potatoes, onions in cream, squash, chicken pie, fruit pudding, sterling sauce, mince, apple, and squash pies, Neapolitan ice cream, fancy cakes, fruit, nuts, and raisins, bonbons, crackers, cheese, and "café noir." But aside from the indulgence of the nineteenth-century sweet tooth with an array of ice cream and candies, and the genteel additions of stylish celery, salted imported almonds, and the fashionable sterling sauce (made with butter, brown sugar, cream, and vanilla or wine), the old Thanksgiving dinner was essentially intact at the end of the nineteenth century.

Thanksgiving Becomes a National Holiday

Compared with the generous number of holidays observed by the European Catholic church, a mere handful of holidays were part of the yearly cycle in early New England. New Year's Day was observed by visiting family and exchanging gifts, particularly in southern New England and New York, where the Dutch had brought the holiday. Washington's birthday was an unofficial national holiday after 1800 (it was made an official holiday in 1885), and many states declared Election Day holidays. For part of the eighteenth and nineteenth centuries, militia training days in the spring and fall were holidays, and the Fourth of July provided an opportunity for toasting, oratory, and noisy celebration. Over the cycle of the year, however, the most important holiday for New Englanders was Thanksgiving.

CELERY

Celery enjoyed a brief spell of fashionable popularity in the last half of the nineteenth century. Expensive, elegant, and in season November through March, it was accorded a special place on the table in its own footed celery glass. Marion Harland, in the *Dinner Year Book,* said that "Celery and Grape Jelly should flank your castor or épergne or whatever may be your centre-piece." A castor was a metal stand, sometimes silver, sometimes plated, that held glass cruets for oil and vinegar, salt and pepper shakers, and sometimes a mustard jar. An épergne was a tall stand, often silver, with branches on which fruit and flowers could be draped decoratively and dramatically. Clearly, celery was prominently displayed.

Miss Harland also said that celery was the "usual accompaniment of roast turkey." Her advice: "Prepare by selecting the blanched [deliberately whitened during the growing process] stalks, scraping off the rust, cutting off all but the youngest and tenderest tops, and laying them in cold water to crisp until wanted for the table."

In 1863, thanks largely to the efforts of New Hampshire's Sarah Josepha Hale, Thanksgiving became an annual national holiday (see page 34). By then, the 1621 harvest celebration of the English colonists and the Wampanoag People had been "discovered" and dubbed "The First Thanksgiving," despite the fact it was neither a first nor a thanksgiving. As the twentieth century approached, Thanksgiving became more widely observed outside its native New England. By then, some of the old animosities from the Civil War were fading and more Southerners observed the day, and as thousands of new immigrants came to the United States, they were initiated into the celebration, too.

Preparing for the Big Day

Energy and enthusiasm were heaped upon the nineteenth-century Thanksgiving celebration, mostly by the women of the household as they cleaned, cooked, and organized for the day. On

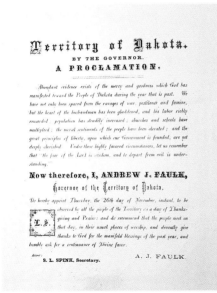

farms, butchering large animals like cattle and swine often preceded the holiday by a week or more, so households were absorbed by the tasks of cutting up meat, salting where appropriate, and making lard and tallow, sausage, and head cheese. All the remaining chores to prepare for winter, like cutting and splitting wood, storing corn for family and animals, making and barreling cider, and wrapping up the harvest, had to be completed by snowfall, which often occurred in the 1800s by Thanksgiving time. Turkeys were killed and chickens dispatched for chicken pie. Pumpkins had to be pared and cooked for sweet pies, and apples peeled and cored, sometimes stewed, for apple pie. Mincemeat-making was a multistep process that yielded pie filling for the holiday and the winter.

As the century wore on and American towns grew, town-dwellers could obtain their turkey and chickens already plucked and ready for stuff-

above right: A Thanksgiving meal in the North around the time of the Civil War. *A Thanksgiving Dinner Among Their Descendants* by W. S. L. Jewett, from *Harper's Weekly,* November 30, 1867. *above left:* Traditionally, each state and territory declared its own Thanksgiving—even after Lincoln created the annual holiday. Thanksgiving Proclamation, North Dakota Territory, November 26, 1868.

Mrs. Hale and the National Holiday

Sarah Josepha Buell Hale was born in New Hampshire in October 1788. She is best known to us as the editor of *Godey's Lady's Book,* a popular nineteenth-century women's magazine, famous for its influential plates showing current fashions in clothing.

Mrs. Hale lobbied hard from 1847 through 1863 to have Thanksgiving declared a national holiday. New Englanders and their descendants, wherever they settled, tended to observe an annual Thanksgiving. Mrs. Hale felt that the celebration brought out the best in people, and possibly under the influence of her own fond recollections of the day and a rising awareness of America's uniqueness, she began to advocate a national observance.

In addition to composing editorials in *Godey's,* her campaign consisted of writing annually to the president, all state governors, and each member of Congress, asking them to consider establishing an annual Thanksgiving nationwide. Her effort finally paid off in 1863, when she was able to convince President Lincoln that a national Thanksgiving might serve to unite the war-torn country. Lincoln established the last Thursday of November as an annual national Thanksgiving holiday. How well observed the holiday was in 1863 is another matter. In the early years after Lincoln's proclamation, the national holiday was unpopular in the South. Promoted as it was by Yankees, and declared when the North was winning, some Southerners, not surprisingly, ignored Lincoln's established day and appointed their own Thanksgivings.

ing at butcher shops or from vendors. Some people could even buy canned pumpkin and squash for their dinner. At the same time there was, among the aspiring middle class at least, a greater effort toward holiday elegance. Housewives with hired help prepared more elaborate menus, baked fancy cakes in addition to dessert pies, turned cranberry jelly into molded dishes, and perhaps attempted a galantine of turkey, boned, stuffed with forcemeat, and glazed with aspic.

But the effort didn't stop there. Cleaning best rooms for company, arranging for overnight guests, and making sure that regular meals arrived on the table daily *before* the great feast were all on the housewives' to-do lists as well. For prosperous families, another important pre-holiday task was the preparation and distribution of food to the poor.

The Big Day

By Thanksgiving Day, anything that could be made ahead was, leaving dinner vegetables to prepare, the bird to stuff and roast, and the gravy to make. By the early 1800s, all-day church attendance had given way to a morning service that allowed for an ample meal in the middle of the day. Some family members went to church, while others stayed home to tend to the dinner. When the service was over, everyone gathered to eat. Among country people, food service was likely to be informal. Harriet Beecher Stowe, no doubt elaborating on her own childhood memories in her novel *Oldtown Folks*, described a long table set up in the kitchen and dishes, "without regard to the French doctrine of courses, . . . all piled together in jovial abundance." Prosperous families with dining rooms, matching sets of dishes, platters, vegetable bowls, tureens, gravy boats, and silver flatware also offered a profusion of dishes on the table at one time, and they did so with considerably more self-conscious style. The Thanksgiving holiday was exactly the special occasion on which to use the fine china.

Some accounts of the day report a blessing on the meal before everyone ate. Conversation sometimes touched upon missing members of the family, those who were far away or who had died since the previous year's gathering. In families where drinking was permitted (the temperance movement was active at the time), as in Caroline King's childhood home in Salem, Massachusetts, "Old family jokes were laughed over, healths were drunk, and toasts given, old songs sung, and friends passed away lovingly remembered." Indoor games, outdoor sports, sleighing, sledding, ice skating, music, and possibly even a dance occupied the balance of the day.

above: Thanksgiving was filled with preparations for servant and mistress alike. Note the impressive cast-iron stove in the background, a thoroughly modern convenience in 1890. *The Day Before Thanksgiving* by Frank O. Small, from *Harper's Weekly*, November 22, 1890.

Why Turkey, Mincemeat, and Plum Pudding at Thanksgiving?

We can easily understand the appearance of squash, pumpkins, turnips, onions, apples, even cranberry sauce. These fruits and vegetables were fresh in the autumn, newly harvested, a natural part of a festive harvest celebration. But turkey, mincemeat, and plum pudding carried other associations that lent meaning to the Thanksgiving holiday.

Turkey

Turkey was usually the most important Thanksgiving meat, to which everything else seemed a side dish. Set at the end of the table before the family patriarch for carving, a large, beautifully browned turkey announced Thanksgiving Day. Large roasted birds had been celebratory meat for centuries by the time Americans added turkey to Thanksgiving. From the Renaissance to the early modern era, swans, herons, cranes, turkeys, pheasants, and other wild and domestic fowl were served to the elite classes. Fowl was delicate fare, considered suitable for the refined tastes of courtiers. Like so many fashions, the taste for fowl at celebrations sifted down from the royalty to the wealthy and eventually the middle classes. Turkey was, by the nineteenth century, simply the most festive meat an average American family could put on the table. To demonstrate charity at Thanksgiving, the prosperous often distributed turkey to workers or poorer relations and neighbors so that fewer people missed out on a fine meal.

Further, turkey had an association with the Pilgrims—who, it was assumed with no explicit proof, *must* have had turkey at the first Thanksgiving. Most Victorians

above: Many different activities took place over the holiday, including homecoming, feasting, dancing, and of course, the after-dinner nap. *Thanksgiving Sketches* by Thomas Nast, from *Harper's Weekly,* December 8, 1866.

A Great Day for Games

In the 1800s, Thanksgiving was a day for sports and games, as it still is in many families. In Connecticut at that time, Grace Denison Wheeler wrote, "After dinner was over the men would go out into the big field near by to play ball or pitch horseshoes or try throwing barrel hoops over a stake to see who could ring the most, the fastest. Even if the day was quite cold, they would be in their shirtsleeves, and heated from the vigorous exercises, they presumably settled their hearty dinner for later in the afternoon they would come in hungry for one of the raised cakes Grandmother had made especially for the occasion with yeast and fruit and many eggs, or to get another piece of pie, with some more good cheese."

Another early New Englander recalled seeing the older generation in a light-hearted mood. Mary Channing observed in New Hampshire in the 1830s: "It was a royal festival; chiefly, and above all because of its afternoon and evening, in which, for once in the whole year, our elders unbent, and in place of the strictness and severity of other days, actually played games!—blind man's bluff, fox and geese, hunt the slipper and twirling the plate." And, of course, there was football. In 1876, only thirteen years after Thanksgiving became a national holiday, the first Thanksgiving Day college football game was held. Yale beat Princeton.

knew that wild turkey abounded in the early years of settlement in America, and as they themselves liked turkey they decided that their forebears had, too. Anyone mindful of the Pilgrim Fathers, though certainly not everyone was, would have enjoyed the idea of eating the same fare as the "founders" of the holiday. Colonists coming to America had indeed found great stores of wild turkeys, and promptly overhunted them. By the nineteenth century, most American Thanksgiving turkeys were domesticated, as they had been in England since the mid-1500s, where turkeys were the most expensive holiday fowl available, far outclassing geese. Little surprise, then, that when Americans chose to celebrate Thanksgiving, turkey reappeared on the table. They simply could not think of a more festive way to go.

Mincemeat

Mincemeat was an important addition to the daily farm diet in the winter as well as to the Thanksgiving celebration. Most butchering was done in the autumn, both to take advantage of

the cold weather for preservation and to avoid having to feed livestock through the winter. Thus the ingredients for mincemeat—bits and scraps of beef or venison, including tongue, neck meat, and feet—were available in November and December. Making mincemeat used up and preserved these scraps for later eating, and the addition of suet (the hard fat from beef), seasonally available apples, and sometimes cider produced a delicious food suitable for celebrations.

But mincemeat also had old associations with Christmas in England. A raised pie filled with mincemeat made in a shape to suggest the manger was an established dish for Christmas by Elizabethan times. It was so thoroughly associated with Christmas that to make a mincemeat pie around December 25 strongly suggested the intention to observe the holiday. When the Puritans rejected Christmas observances, a late-December mincemeat pie became suspect. But it was one thing to give up Christmas and quite another to give up the old favorite mincemeat pie. The Puritans and their descendants happily assigned the pie to Thanksgiving.

At more elegant dinners in the eighteenth century, a mincemeat pie, more savory than sweet, might appear on the table with meat in the first course. By the nineteenth century, however, even though it still contained meat, it was considered a dessert and so slid to the end of the meal.

Plum Pudding

Plum pudding had a similar association with festivity, but a somewhat less pronounced Christmas connection. As a rich, flavorful dish, usually made with suet and full of raisins and currants, it too may have been part of the first course in earlier times, but, like mincemeat pie, it ended up among the desserts in the 1800s.

Pies

It would be hard to underestimate the importance of pies at Thanksgiving. Like mincemeat, pies were a Thanksgiving tradition with roots in England. Many memoirs of nineteenth-

above: Scenes depicting the Pilgrims were a popular subject of twentieth-century commemorative plates.

above: This re-created tableau of John and Priscilla Alden, circa 1910, is typical of the romantic view of the Pilgrims in the colonial revival period.

CHRISTMAS COMES TO NEW ENGLAND

Christmas, the premier English holiday, was deliberately not celebrated in New England until the middle of the nineteenth century; it even had been briefly outlawed in Boston. The Puritans of New England found no biblical precedent for celebrating Christ's birthday on December 25 or any other day, and they felt that too much secular feasting and mirth accompanied a day that, if marked at all, should be a religious observance only. Christmas was not the only holiday dispensed with in Puritan New England. Easter, May Day, and a host of other popular English celebrations were deliberately left behind as well.

But by the 1870s, more and more New Englanders, and their descendants across the country, were observing Christmas. The strict Protestantism of early New England gradually relaxed through the seventeenth and eighteenth centuries, and so did the prohibition on Christmas celebrations. New, attractive, and largely secular aspects of the holiday, like Santa Claus, stockings hung by the chimney, and Christmas trees, took hold in the popular imagination. Elsewhere in the country, Episcopalians and Catholics had observed Christmas continuously, and European immigrants from countries like Germany, that had strong Christmas traditions, had kept the holiday flourishing. New Englanders were drawn in slowly, and by the nineteenth century's end, most Christians observed some form of the Christmas holiday, complete with a dinner menu remarkably similar to Thanksgiving's.

century childhoods tell of massive pie-bakings in advance of the holiday. In addition to donating turkeys to the less fortunate, prosperous households often gave away pies, or at least the ingredients for them. Other households made pies in anticipation of company to entertain before, on, and after the holiday. Some took advantage of cold pantries and closets to lay away pies that might even freeze but would be ready to pull out and warm up for company in the ensuing winter.

In the work of making all those pies, if we believe the memoirs, children cheerfully pitched in, helping pound and sift spices, taking seeds out of raisins, peeling apples, and more. Mary Channing wrote, "We were willing helpers in all the preparations—the chopping of meat and apples, the picking over of currants and raisins for mincemeat pies."

Thanksgiving Shapes Up

By the end of the nineteenth century, Thanksgiving was thoroughly entrenched as an American holiday. The turkey was firmly lodged in a place of honor, and even if pumpkin pie was never eaten at any other time, it, too, was indispensable. Americans seemed to agree that Thanksgiving was the ideal time to go see "the folks," and once dinner was over, or while it was being made, a football game was a terrific way to pass the time. But more changes were in store for this great American holiday in the twentieth century.

above: A sophisticated urban nineteenth-century Thanksgiving dinner. *Thanksgiving Day in New York—As It Was* by W. T. Smedley, from *Harper's Weekly*, November 28, 1891.

Thanksgiving and the American Century

Without a doubt, the turbulent twentieth century left as large a mark on the Thanksgiving menu as the formative nineteenth. The holiday menu Americans inherited at the beginning of the twentieth century was the simple celebratory harvest food of New England Yankees. This rustic menu was not without controversy. At the end of the nineteenth century, some women's magazines were touting the delicate, sophisticated Thanksgiving foods eaten by the wealthy Victorians at "refined tables" in northern cities. Staunch supporters of the traditional holiday menu would have none of this and waged a counter-campaign in their own magazines, looking back with nostalgia to the idealized Thanksgivings of their grandparents. In the end, of course, the rustic feast of New England farmers triumphed, and twentieth-century cooks inherited many dishes that still remain at the heart of the traditional holiday meal today—delights like roast turkey, bread stuffing, cranberry sauce, mashed potatoes, turnips, winter squash, celery, creamed onions, pumpkin pie, and apple pie. But as tastes and cooking practices changed over the course of the century, other dishes that were part of the traditional bill of fare have largely fallen away. Modern American cooks rarely make chicken pies, steamed plum puddings, and mincemeat pie, yet all of these dishes were popular Thanksgiving foods in the eighteenth and nineteenth centuries. But while we might regret a handful of wonderful heirloom dishes falling by the wayside, the twentieth century brought new foods, recipes, and cooking styles to the Thanksgiving table.

In the last century, enormous changes in gender roles, kitchen technology, transportation, food preservation, and agriculture permanently affected the way all Americans eat and live. After World War II, women joined the workforce in ever-increasing numbers, changing their larger role in society as well as reducing their time available for everyday cooking and holiday meal preparation. Processed foods became an increasingly common convenience for home cooks, and the food industry began to dominate the American kitchen and palate. Small local markets filled with regional and seasonal fare gave way to supermarkets crammed with mass-produced foods. Small family farms, once the backbone of the nation's economy, all but disap-

left: The Winsor family Thanksgiving dinner, 1882.

peared from the agricultural landscape. There was an astounding increase in the number and variety of recipes available as well, as thousands of new cookbooks and dozens of cooking and women's magazines flourished in the marketplace. In the second half of the century, television (including the twenty-four-hour Food Network) and the Internet emerged as new and popular sources for distributing recipes and spreading food trends across the nation.

Changes in Kitchen Technology

The technological revolution that had begun in the late 1800s completely transformed the American kitchen by the end of the 1900s. At the turn of the twentieth century, kitchens were equipped with iceboxes and housewives cooked on stoves fueled by coal, wood, or oil. Some still cooked at open fireplace hearths. After 1910, gas ranges, and several years later electric ones, began to replace the older stoves. By 1920, electrical appliances, including skillets, toasters, mixers, waffle irons, chafing dishes, and coffee percolators, began appearing in urban middle-

❧ "FRANKSGIVING" ❧

Abraham Lincoln declared the first of our modern annual Thanksgivings in 1863. Every succeeding president followed suit, but it wasn't until 1941, after a national controversy, that the holiday and official date of celebration became law. Retailers asked Franklin D. Roosevelt to declare November 23, 1939—the next to the last Thursday—as Thanksgiving for that year. Retailers believed a late-falling Thanksgiving (it would have been held on November 30 that year) would dampen holiday sales, since the traditional shopping season would be so short. Roosevelt agreed to their request, and the announcement—which was front-page news across the country—resulted in a storm of controversy from traditionalists, Republicans (Roosevelt was a Democrat), and football fans. In 1939, some Americans celebrated Thanksgiving on the 23rd (dubbed "Franksgiving"), and others kept the "true" holiday on the last Thursday (the 30th). Some celebrated both! The holiday controversy raged again in 1940 and 1941, as early Franksgivings were again declared. Finally, in 1941, Roosevelt admitted that moving the holiday date had been a mistake and, on November 26, he signed the Congressional bill that designated the fourth Thursday in November as the official Thanksgiving holiday.

class homes (though many rural areas had to wait for electricity until after World War II). In the late 1920s and the following decade, refrigerators (some of which included freezers) replaced iceboxes in many American kitchens. More recent additions include microwaves, automatic dishwashers, Crock-Pots, food processors, bread machines, countertop grills, juicers, convection ovens, and a host of specialty appliances that sometimes seem to border on the ridiculous. (Does anyone *really* need a hot dog cooker that cooks "6 hot dogs in 60 seconds"?) Novelty appliances aside, the majority of these innovations were aimed at reducing the drudgery of kitchen work and making the preparation (and cleanup) of meals faster and easier.

Of course, many of these improvements affected the way the Thanksgiving meal was prepared. Timesaving appliances like food processors and mixers made short work of any number of holiday tasks. Gas and electric ovens, adjusted with the turn of a dial, provided steady, reliable heat. Meat thermometers ensured that even inexperienced cooks could perfectly roast a turkey. Refrigerators and freezers revolutionized the way Americans purchased, prepared, and stored food. Prepared holiday favorites made their way into the freezer section of the local market and could be purchased at any time of the year anywhere in the country. The Thanksgiving holiday and the notion of preserving food, or "putting by the harvest," were no longer connected. In fact, the entire Thanksgiving meal could be assembled without a single homemade element. There is no doubt that these twentieth-century labor-saving introductions significantly reduced the work of preparing the holiday meal. Thanksgiving preparations, which had formerly taken days and involved the whole family, could now be accomplished in a matter of hours. As wonderful as many of these innovations were, one cannot help but look back to holiday descriptions from earlier centuries and envy the sense of camaraderie and connectedness that accompanied the long work of preparing the Thanksgiving meal. Even so, it *is* hard to wax nostalgic about some family Thanksgiving activities, like plucking and gutting the holiday bird!

New Foods and Technologies

Changes in food technology that began in the middle of the nineteenth century gained momentum in the twentieth, greatly affecting the daily food of Americans. Food became big business as a growing number of companies mass-produced and mass-marketed processed food products to eager consumers who sought freedom from the work of cooking. (Many of these same consumers had employed cooks earlier in the century.) Over the course of the twentieth century, the processed-food trend accelerated, and grocery stores were filled with standardized canned and packaged brand-name foods that became the backbone of everyday meals for many Americans (the 1950s being the high point—or low point, depending on your way of thinking—of this sort of cooking). Thanks to Clarence Birdseye, frozen foods appeared in the 1930s. In that decade,

Check your newspaper around Thanksgiving and you will undoubtedly find a photograph of the president of the United States on the White House lawn with a turkey. Since 1947, the National Turkey Federation has presented one live turkey and two dressed turkeys (plucked and ready to cook) to the president. In 1947, Harry Truman was the first to receive the honor. According to the Truman Library, his papers contain no indication that he pardoned that first live turkey. In fact, the official pardoning of the national turkey did not begin until 1989 with George H. W. Bush.

The turkeys to be presented for pardoning are chosen in August (based on size, plumage, and poise) and then undergo six months of training to make sure they are on their best behavior in November. Part of this training involves exposing the birds to men in dark business suits so there are no surprises during the fateful meeting of president and turkey. The lucky pardoned turkey is retired to a local zoo to live out its days.

above: During the administration of Harry S. Truman, the National Turkey Federation began its annual presentation of a turkey to the president, a custom that continues to this day.

Birdseye (and food giant General Foods) offered free freezers to grocery stores as an enticement to carry "Birds Eye Frosted Foods," and in the 1940s he effectively marketed frozen vegetables as a better alternative to canned. After World War II, frozen foods of all sorts (including the Thanksgiving turkey) became widely available, and within a few years they seemed indispensable in American kitchens. All of these innovations, plus advances in transportation, meant that many seasonal and regional food limitations became a thing of the past.

Many new and popular Thanksgiving favorites grew out of these changes. Late nineteenth- and twentieth-century food inventions like cream cheese, marshmallows, frozen piecrusts, corn syrup, and canned products such as cranberry sauce, pumpkin, olives, and condensed soups are key ingredients in such twentieth-century holiday recipes as pumpkin cheesecake and green bean casserole. Time-saving convenience foods like stuffing mixes (this section seems to expand daily at the grocery store), frozen pies, and nondairy whipped toppings became part of the holiday tradition for some families. Advertisers (who also proliferated at a remarkable rate!) were quick to connect their clients' food products to the holiday in the hope of boosting sales, and November magazines bristled with holiday tie-in ads for everything from marshmallows to mushroom soup.

New Ways of Thinking About Food

The holiday spreads from women's magazines and cookbooks in the first half of the twentieth century don't vary much from menu to menu. No doubt women made subtle choices based on their household budget and personal taste, some choosing the more economical roast chicken instead of turkey or opting for parsnips instead of turnips. But still, these menus give a sense of a *prescribed* bill of fare—as though one *ought* to eat this particular array of foods to have a true American Thanksgiving. This sense of a prescribed menu persists today, to some degree. For instance, few people choose to entirely forgo the turkey and cranberry sauce; in fact, 95 percent of Americans eat turkey on Thanksgiving Day.

The dishes that surround the turkey, however, have become much more variable over the course of the century. These developments in the traditional menu started out slowly with the addition of trendy new foods like gelatin salads and stuffed celery in the first decades of the 1900s. By the end of the century, newcomers like curried pumpkin bisque, cranberry chutney, pumpkin cheesecake, and chocolate pecan pie reflected the staggering culinary changes. In the last half of the century, a world of food had opened up for average, middle-class Americans. The population had changed, becoming more ethnically diverse. Americans, no matter their ethnic background, ate and appreciated the foods of other cultures. Imported ingredients from all over the world made their way into neighborhood markets at affordable prices. International travel, including wartime service overseas, further broadened the tastes of the nation. For many, cooking became an enjoyable activity (at least part of the time), and cookbook writers like James Beard, Julia Child, and Alice Waters, to name just a few, helped expand the culinary world. Inevitably, these changes meant that dishes like the mincemeat pie and plum pudding, popular at the beginning of the twentieth century, gave way on the Thanksgiving table to modern holiday recipes better suited to new American tastes.

❧ FAMILY REUNION ❧

More than any other holiday, Thanksgiving has evolved as a time to gather together. On Christmas most Americans stay at home, but on Thanksgiving, many pack up and leave home to spend the holiday with relatives and friends. This is nearly as old a custom of the day as having turkey and pumpkin pie.

The reunion tradition arose in the early eighteenth century as families began dispersing across New England to settle on the frontiers of New England: western Massachusetts, Vermont, New Hampshire, and Maine. Gradually, before and after the Revolutionary War, New Englanders pressed into New York State, Ohio, and even parts of the southern colonies and territories. In the nineteenth century, hundreds of New Englanders went west during the Gold Rush and subsequent westward migrations. And as Boston, New York, and other towns grew into cities, young people left farms to join businesses or to work in industries in urban centers. Thanksgiving was the time people chose for family reunion, to go back to the old homestead for a visit. It still is.

Talking Turkey

The twentieth century also saw significant changes to the centerpiece of the holiday table, the turkey. If the English colonists and the Wampanoag ate turkey in 1621, it was the wild turkey still found in many parts of the country today. These birds were close to extinction a century ago, though populations have recovered nicely. (Wild turkeys are smaller, gamier, and a bit tougher than domestic turkeys, but they are delicious in their own right.) Later Americans raised their own birds or purchased them from local butchers or poultry farmers. Today, the vast majority of Americans purchase fresh or frozen turkeys at the supermarket. These turkeys come from large poultry processing plants and distributors like Butterball.

The colonists would hardly recognize the buxom bird sitting on most of our Thanksgiving tables. In the past fifty years, one particular breed of turkey, the broad-breasted Large White, has completely dominated the marketplace. These turkeys are bred for their plentiful white meat, making them irresistible to white-meat-loving Americans. Today, all large-scale turkey farmers raise the Large White turkey, and specialty feeds and management practices have "improved" the variety, creating a fast-growing, top-heavy bird that reaches maturity between four and nine months of age. The absolute dominance of this bird has forced older breeds from the market. These distinctive and delicious breeds of turkey, including the Narragansett, the Bourbon Red, the American Bronze, and the Jersey Buff, were in danger of disappearing entirely from American farms until organizations like the American Livestock Breeds Conservancy and Slow Foods USA recently began to help small farmers bring them back to the Thanksgiving table. (For information about purchasing wild or heritage breed turkeys for your holiday table, visit www.localharvest.org or heritagefoodsusa.com.)

In the second half of the twentieth century, some Americans changed the way they cooked their holiday bird. Oven roasting is still far and away the most popular method of cooking the turkey, but in recent decades, more than a few people have opted to cook their turkey outdoors.

✺ TOFU TURKEY ✺

The American vegetarian movement began in the middle of the nineteenth century and began picking up steam over a century later. By the 1980s, tofu could be found in every mainstream American supermarket, and in 1992 the first tofu turkey was produced and marketed by Fresh Tofu, Inc. Of course, the Thanksgiving meal in many ways is vegetarian-friendly. It features loads of interesting vegetables and dressings that are easily adapted to suit non-meat eaters. If they avoid the turkey and gravy, most vegetarians can happily fill their plate. The inventor of tofu turkey, Gary Abramowitz, relates that despite all of this there was still something missing: "For twenty years of Thanksgiving dinners as a vegetarian, I attended my family gatherings always feeling a little left out and a little unsatisfied. My meal consisted of wonderful vegetable side dishes, and although they were lovingly prepared and quite delicious—my feast needed a focus, a centerpiece. The first tofu turkey was created to fill that void. It was a whopping 8 pounds and measured 14 inches across!" Now that's a lot of tofu!

above: A World War II soldier helps his mother prepare the holiday meal in this 1945 painting by Norman Rockwell, *Thanksgiving: Mother and Son Peeling Potatoes*. Another famous Rockwell Thanksgiving painting, *Freedom from Want*, features several generations of a family gathered around a holiday table.

People have been cooking outdoors over fires for thousands of years. By Western standards, progress meant moving the whole process of meal preparation indoors, but outdoor backyard barbecuing became a new national pastime for the men of suburban America after World War II. The barbecue boom shows no sign of slowing down as we proceed into the twenty-first century. It was inevitable that barbecue enthusiasts would turn their attention to the Thanksgiving turkey—particularly in the South and South-west, where roasting a turkey for hours indoors tends to make the house a tad too warm. More recently, outdoor turkey cookery has expanded still more to smoking and deep-frying. The latter technique is particularly popular in the South, where it originated. Lowering a 12-pound turkey into gallons of boiling peanut oil can be a tricky maneuver, but the result is worth the advance planning; you get an extremely moist turkey done in record time—that 12-pound turkey cooks in less than 45 minutes!

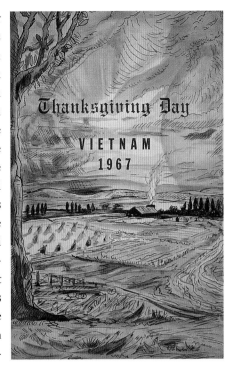

Thanksgiving During Wartime

During both world wars, housewives on the home front were asked by the government to ration a number of foods, including sugar, wheat, coffee, meat, butter, cheese, and canned goods. At Thanksgiving time, magazines, cookbooks, and newspapers gave recipes for ration-friendly "Patriotic Thanksgivings" like molasses-sweetened pumpkin pies and wheat-free breads. Many families ate Thanksgiving chicken dinners so that soldiers overseas could have turkey. To make sure there was no interruption of the war effort, employees in key wartime factories worked on Thanksgiving Day and postponed their holiday meal to the end of the day's shift. During World War II, Macy's department store canceled its Thanksgiving parade to conserve gasoline and rubber for the war effort.

In the twentieth century, against what may seem like overwhelming obstacles, the American military has gone to great lengths to make sure that servicemen and -women are served a

above: While grateful for the holiday meal, many veterans recall that Thanksgiving was one of the toughest days to be separated from family. Thanksgiving Menu, Vietnam, 1967.

traditional roast turkey dinner on Thanksgiving Day. Thanksgiving dinners have gone to the front by helicopter, jeep, boat, and mule. According to *Thanksgiving,* by Diana Karter Appelbaum, Thanksgiving dinners in 1942 were literally hurled across a river in Italy to waiting soldiers when downed bridges made travel by jeep impossible. World War II continued to affect food even after it ended. Many servicemen and -women returned home with a new appreciation for foreign foods. In addition, the need to feed an army scattered across the world had led to food and food packaging innovations (like ready-to-eat meals, powdered orange juice, and dehydrated potatoes) that soon made their way to domestic store shelves. Factories built to produce food for the wartime effort turned their attention to the challenge of making these processed foods indispensable to Americans housewives.

New Thanksgiving Pastimes

Twentieth-century Thanksgiving innovations were not limited to the table. In the formative years of the holiday, dinner was planned around morning church services. For some time now, in many households Thanksgiving dinner is scheduled around football games and parades.

In 1876, the newly formed Intercollegiate Football Association scheduled its championship game for Thanksgiving Day. By the 1890s, the league's championship game, held on the Polo Grounds of New York City, was a premier event in the New York social season. Area churches made sure that Thanksgiving services ended well before kickoff time. Other colleges and high schools followed suit and by the start of the twentieth century thousands of football games were played on Thanksgiving Day across the country, usually between traditional rivals. The custom was not without its critics; in 1883, a *New York Herald* article declared that "Thanksgiving Day is no longer a solemn festival to God for mercies given.... It is a holiday granted by the State and the Nation to see a game of football."

In 1934, professional football followed the Thanksgiving example when George Richards, owner of both the Detroit Lions and a radio station, scheduled a game between his team and the Chicago Bears at the University of Detroit's stadium. By networking a number of radio stations, he was able to broadcast the game across the country, and another Thanksgiving tradition was born. (Chicago won 19–16.) Today, millions of households around the country watch games played by the National Football League's Detroit Lions, the Dallas Cowboys, or both, and arrange their dinner plans accordingly. For millions of Americans, it wouldn't be Thanksgiving without NFL football.

New York's Thanksgiving parades go much further back than today's popular Macy's celebration. From the 1780s until just before World War II, riotous groups (called *fantastical companies*) of

left: In the twentieth century, the Macy's Thanksgiving Day Parade and its giant balloons became a new and popular element of the holiday.

young working-class men from different New York neighborhoods dressed in flamboyant costumes made their way through the streets on Thanksgiving morning. The origin of the Thanksgiving custom is obscure, and there seemed to be little point in these gatherings—other than good-natured roistering on a day off from work (which were few and far between when the custom began).

The Macy's tradition began in 1924 and was originally called "The Macy's Christmas Parade." Its origin is credited to Macy's employees, many of them European immigrants, who wanted to celebrate the holiday with a European-style parade featuring costumes, clowns, zoo animals, bands, and floats. The store's employees may have lobbied for the parade holiday, but Macy's executives also had a ready eye toward encouraging Christmas shopping in the weeks that followed Thanksgiving. After all, Santa's annual presence at the end of the parade was a clear signal to all that the holiday shopping season had officially begun. Over the twentieth century, the parade continued to grow and evolve. In 1927, the first of the giant balloons—Felix the Cat—was added, and in the 1950s the parade acquired a national television audience that continues to this day.

New Ways of Thinking About Thanksgiving

Thanksgiving came under scrutiny after the social upheaval of the 1960s and 1970s. Many social activists questioned whether Thanksgiving was appropriate in a nation with so many poor

and homeless. People for the Ethical Treatment of Animals (PETA) campaigned for turkey-free Thanksgiving dinners. The most prominent non-Thanksgiving, however, is the National Day of Mourning, created by Native People for whom successful European colonization is certainly no cause for celebration. In 1970, Wampanoag leader Frank James was invited by Massachusetts officials to speak at the 350th anniversary of the landing of the Pilgrims. His speech was read in advance by officials, considered "too controversial," and edited. James refused to deliver the censored speech. In response, the United American Indians of New England (UAINE) called for a National Day of Mourning, held in Plymouth on Thanksgiving Day, at which James delivered his original speech. The National Day of Mourning has been held annually in Plymouth since 1970, continuing to serve as an important forum for Native speakers to focus public awareness on Native issues and history.

above: Russell Means, from the Oglala/Lakota Nations, is an important voice and leader in the American Indian Movement (AIM). He spoke at the first National Day of Mourning in Plymouth, Massachusetts. *Photograph from the* Patriot Ledger, *November 27, 1970.*

The Melting Pot:
Food Traditions from America
and Beyond

"What do you *eat* for Thanksgiving?" The New England Yankees who created the holiday would be astonished at the range of answers to this question today. They probably wouldn't be very pleased, either. For them, the holiday menu was not a thing to trifle with or to adapt according to one's own culinary traditions. In fact, at the end of the nineteenth century and well into the twentieth, Thanksgiving and the "official" Yankee holiday menu were seen as a means of encouraging the Americanization of the millions of new immigrants to the United States. For a fast-growing nation in the wake of the divisive Civil War, Thanksgiving also offered a much-needed sense of shared tradition and an appealing national identity.

By the last few decades of the twentieth century, however, the purpose and meaning of the holiday had changed. Today, the Thanksgiving holiday is still seen as a means of uniting a diverse America, but it has also become a means of expressing one's background and individuality. The wonderful reality of the modern American Thanksgiving is that while there are seemingly sacred or untouchable elements in the holiday bill of fare like turkey, cranberries, and pumpkin pie, there is no longer a single "authentic" menu. Each family has its own definition of what makes a "real" Thanksgiving. And today, an infinite number of menu variations reflect the complex American tapestry of regional heritage, family traditions, ethnic background, and even social class.

Making Thanksgiving Their Own

There is much about Thanksgiving that appeals to people of every ethnic background, especially the practice of sharing a feast with family and friends. For many non-European immigrants, however, roasting a whole turkey is a new and not especially appealing culinary challenge. Indeed, when viewed from the vibrant food cultures of the Far and Near East, the traditional American Thanksgiving menu can look, well, pretty bland and dull. Some first-generation immigrants choose to forgo the bird and trimmings entirely; they honor the sentiment of holiday with the celebratory foods of their own culinary heritage. A traditional

American Thanksgiving dinner is uncommon in the recently arrived Cambodian community in Lowell, Massachusetts, for instance.

For other immigrants, turkey *is* on their Thanksgiving menu (often because the children learn at school that turkey is a Thanksgiving necessity), but it may be inserted into a traditional meal. In many first- and second-generation Italian American families, for instance, turkey dinner is the main course, but only after traditional antipasto and pasta courses have been served, and the dessert course includes favorite specialties from home. Often, families with strong ethnic identities prepare the traditional American turkey using the seasonings and preparations of their cultural heritage, as is illustrated by the Lebanese rice dressing and Indian-spiced turkey recipes in the recipe section of this book. This notion of a festive Thanksgiving meal that includes familiar dishes and traditions from the "old country" was certainly not part of the holiday experience for newcomers to America in the nineteenth and early twentieth centuries, however.

A Nation of Immigrants

Before 1820, the population of the United States was predominately Western European (English, Scotch-Irish, Dutch, German, French, and Scottish) and African (forcibly brought as slaves beginning in 1619). In the middle of the century, new immigrants arrived as news of the

Gold Rush, and the general prosperity to be had in America, reached Asia and Europe. Among the new immigrants were Irish (many of them Catholic), escaping the nightmare of the potato famine; German peasants, displaced by economic changes; Scandinavians; Canadians; and the first Chinese immigrants. The largest waves of immigration took place between 1880 and 1920. The immigrants came from all over the world: southern and eastern Europe, the Middle East, the Mediterranean, and Canada. Italians came by the millions, as did Eastern European and Russian Jews who were fleeing pogroms at home. Armenians fled massacres in Turkey, and Mexicans escaped the Revolution. All told, more than 27 million people entered the United States during this time (including 20 million processed through Ellis Island after it opened in 1892), seeking refuge from poverty, war, and persecution. Later in the twentieth century, immigrants continued to

above: From 1880 to 1920, the largest wave of immigration as of then took place, with 27 million immigrants entering the United States. This undated photograph shows immigrants newly arrived at Ellis Island, New York.

"The American Thing to Do"

Nigisti Hadgu came to Boston from Eritrea (northeast Africa on the Red Sea) in 1983. Mrs. Hadgu and her cousin Elsa Bahta, who arrived in 1997, celebrate the American Thanksgiving holiday together with their extended family. Their holiday meal is a mixture of American and Eritrean dishes. Mrs. Hadgu initially made Etritrean foods instead of the traditional turkey. Once her children were in school and learned all about Thanksgiving dinner, turkey became part of the meal, too. Now their Thanksgiving dinner includes apple pie, cheesecake, and a turkey stuffed with a spicy bread stuffing with Eritrean flavors like fried onions, garlic, and green pepper. Another American favorite, lasgana, is on the table as well. In addition to this "American" fare, the adults savor their favorite Eritrean dishes, including a spicy chicken stew called *tsebhi derho*, which is eaten with a traditional flat bread. Mrs. Hadgu's holiday is representative of the way immigrants from across the world both honor the sentiment of the Thanksgiving holiday and make it their own.

come from all over the world, including large numbers from the nations of sub-Saharan Africa, the Caribbean (Cuba, the Dominican Republic, Haiti), and southern Asia (India, the Philippines, Vietnam, Korea, and Cambodia).

Despite the bold words of welcome on the Statue of Liberty, earlier immigrants (Protestants from Western Europe) felt threatened by the rising tide of arrivals from Asia and the Catholic southern and eastern European countries. In the last decades of the nineteenth century, anti-immigrant sentiment became pervasive, particularly in the northern cities where many of the new immigrants lived and worked. After 1880, Congress passed several laws that limited immigration from certain nations; the Chinese Exclusion Act severely restricted immigration from China, and literacy tests and laws banning the immigration of paupers became the means of keeping out other immigrant groups. After World War I, prejudices and a fear of "foreign agitators" led to new restrictive laws, including 1924's National Origins Act. This law set quotas that blatantly discriminated against eastern and southern Europeans and Asians, and it was not repealed until 1965.

Reformers, Immigrants, and Thanksgiving

Not all "old stock" Americans were anti-immigrant, however. Many nineteenth- and early-twentieth-century reformers directed their considerable efforts at helping the new immigrants fit in and "become American," usually by abandoning their cultural heritage. The Thanksgiving holiday provided a perfect opportunity for instruction. In settlement houses and factories, adult immigrants were instructed in the major elements of American history. In these lessons, the highly romanticized nineteenth-century story of the "First Thanksgiving" and example of the impossibly virtuous "Pilgrims" (who were presented as "the first immigrants") were used to teach new immigrants lessons about American history and values.

The Thanksgiving menu provided yet another chance for instruction in becoming American. The familiar foods of many new immigrants—thought by "oldcomers" to be spicy, difficult to digest, and overly complex—were also an early focus of these reformers' concerted effort. Home economists and domestic scientists conducted cooking classes to instruct immigrants to set aside their traditional foods and prepare "American" foods like Thanksgiving dinner. These well-intentioned reformers were ultimately unsuccessful in achieving this goal. Instead, over the course of the twentieth century, many "ethnic" foods have entered the American mainstream, and many formerly "foreign" ingredients are now household staples (the once reviled garlic, for instance).

Educators and reformers also turned their attention to the children of the immigrants.

❧ Lasagna and Thanksgiving ❧

One of the most surprising items on the modern Thanksgiving menu is lasagna—and it isn't just on the tables of Italian Americans. Recent immigrants from Eritrea, Bosnia, Trinidad, and India all mentioned that lasagna was a favorite part of their Thanksgiving meal. Lasagna, which came to the United States with immigrant Italians, was not always an American favorite. Some twentieth-century Americans first savored the dish in big-city Italian restaurants in the 1920s, but lasagna did not become popular at the American dinner table until the 1960s. In recent decades, lasagna has become so integrated into the landscape of American food that newcomers perceive it as American—and therefore as suitable for Thanksgiving as turkey and cranberry sauce.

By the beginning of the twentieth century, the Pilgrims and the Thanksgiving holiday were used to teach children how to be good citizens and about the blessings of American freedom. Each November, in classrooms across the country, students participated in Thanksgiving pageants (usually dressed in stereotypical Pilgrim and Indian dress), sang songs about Thanksgiving ("We gather together to ask the Lord's blessing"), and built log cabins (meant to represent the homes of the Pilgrims). Immigrant children also learned that *all* Americans ate turkey for

Thanksgiving dinner. The last lesson was especially effective; the recollections of most immigrant children in the twentieth century include stories of rushing home after school in November to beg their parents to buy and roast a turkey for a holiday dinner. The pleas of children who wanted to fit in worked better than any reformer's cooking classes, and many immigrant families did choose to celebrate the holiday with a turkey.

Not every immigrant family was receptive to the Thanksgiving holiday, however. Many Catholic immigrants were leery of what they perceived to be a Protestant holiday, while many Jews saw Thanksgiving as a Christian holiday. Both of these perceptions were true, considering the roots of the holiday. By the middle of the nineteenth century, though, Thanksgiving had largely moved away from its religious roots and become a secular domestic holiday honoring hearth and home. Over the course of the twentieth century, the nation became increasingly multi-ethnic, and today the idea of a contradiction between having a strong ethnic identity and being an American has much less force. This is borne out every November, when the richly varied ingredients of many culinary traditions join the traditional nineteenth-century turkey and cranberries to express the diverse character of the country. Today, for many immigrants, the act of celebrating Thanksgiving is ultimately imbued with a sense of being American.

above: Ellis Island opened in 1892, and more than 20 million immigrants were processed there. This aerial view of New York Harbor was taken on June 1, 1933.

Local and Regional Thanksgiving Traditions

The classic Thanksgiving menu of turkey, cranberries, pumpkin pie, and root vegetables is based on New England fall harvests. In the nineteenth century, as the holiday spread across the country, local cooks modified the menu both by choice ("this is what we like to eat") and by necessity ("this is what we have to eat"). Today, many Americans delight in giving regional produce, recipes, and seasonings a place on the Thanksgiving table. In New Mexico, chiles and other southwestern flavors are used in stuffing, while on the Chesapeake Bay, the local favorite, crab, often shows up as a holiday appetizer or as an ingredient in dressing. In Minnesota, the turkey might be stuffed with wild rice, and in Washington State, locally grown hazelnuts are featured in stuffing and desserts. In Indiana, persimmon puddings are a favorite Thanksgiving dessert, and in Key West, Key lime pie joins pumpkin pie on the holiday table. Some specialties have even become ubiquitous regional additions to local Thanksgiving menus; in Baltimore, for instance, it is common to find sauerkraut alongside the Thanksgiving turkey.

Most of these regional variations have remained largely a local phenomenon, a means of connecting and honoring with local harvests and specialty foods. However, this is not true of influential southern Thanksgiving trends, which have had a tremendous impact on the twentieth-century Thanksgiving menu.

❧ TURDUCKEN ANYONE? ❧

While deep-frying and grilling are both popular southern treatments for the Thanksgiving turkey, in Louisiana a novel method of cooking and serving three different birds at once has become popular at holiday time. Turducken (or turducken) is a Cajun specialty that consists of three boned birds and three types of stuffing. In Paul Prudhomme's recipe (which can be found on his website, www.chefpaul.com), a 20- to 25-pound turkey is stuffed with a 4- to 5-pound duckling that is stuffed with a 3- to 4-pound chicken. Oyster dressing is placed inside the chicken, andouille (a spicy Cajun sausage) dressing is placed between the chicken and the duck, and corn bread dressing goes between the duck and the turkey. If the thirteen pages of directions and the two days of preparation are a bit daunting, a half-dozen outfits in southern Louisiana will ship you a preassembled turducken that you can roast in your own oven (www.cajungrocer.com or www.farmpac.com).

Thanksgiving Traditions from the American South

In spite of its Yankee roots, Thanksgiving became popular in the South in the late nineteenth century. In the years just before the Civil War, southern governors fell in with the rest of the nation, formalizing the autumn holiday. Supporters of the Union in both the North and South hoped a national Thanksgiving holiday would help bind its fraying edges. Other southerners disliked that some of the northern proponents of the holiday were also abolitionists. After the war, the national holiday met with some resistance. According to Diane Karter Appelbaum's *Thanksgiving,* in 1865 at least one governor, Oran Milo Roberts of Texas, chose not to proclaim Thanksgiving, declaring that it was "a damned Yankee institution." Within a few years, however, southern magazines and newspapers were full of the same Thanksgiving recipes and advice as their northern counterparts. But southerners were not content to adopt the Yankee menu wholesale. Corn, sweet potatoes, and pork form the backbone of traditional southern home cooking, and these staple foods provided the main ingredients in southern Thanksgiving additions like ham, sweet potato casseroles, pies and puddings, and corn bread dressing. Other popular southern contributions include ambrosia (a layered fruit salad traditionally made with citrus fruits and coconut; some more recent recipes use minimarshmallows and canned fruits), biscuits, a host of vegetable casseroles, and even macaroni and cheese. Unlike the traditional New England menu, with its mince, apple, and pumpkin pie dessert course, southerners added a range and selection of desserts unknown in northern dining rooms, including regional cakes, pies, puddings, and cobblers too numerous to mention. Many of these Thanksgiving menu additions spread across the country with relocating southerners. Southern cookbooks (of which there are hundreds) and magazines also helped popularize many of these dishes in places far beyond their southern roots. Some, like sweet potato casserole, pecan pie, and corn bread dressing, have become as expected on the Thanksgiving table as turkey and cranberry sauce.

PART II

The Recipes

STARTERS:
Appetizers, Salads, and Soups

Stuffed Celery

Celery is a Thanksgiving inheritance from the 1800s, when it was a fancy new food worthy of grand presentation on the holiday table in a specially made celery vase. (Read more about this on page 32.) By the 1950s, celery was filled with cream cheese and moved from the formal celery glass to the relish tray, where it was accompanied by pitted black olives, stuffed green olives, sweet and dill pickles, pickled watermelon, and radish roses.

Mild, soft cheeses called *cream cheese* have been around for centuries. The widely known American cream cheese used to stuff celery (and make New York–style cheesecake) was created in 1872. In 1880, Philadelphia Brand cream cheese came to the market, and later innovations included the familiar foil packaging and pasteurization. Cream cheese became a huge hit in the early twentieth century. Cookbooks from the 1920s and 1930s frequently include recipes for celery stuffed with cream cheese, often flavored with blue cheese. Here are some favorite holiday variations on the classic filling. Each recipe generously fills 12 stalks of washed celery (a 1-pound package), well dried and cut into 3-inch lengths.

Chutney and Cream Cheese Filling

⅓ cup chutney, any type, finely chopped
1 8-ounce package cream cheese, softened
¼ cup finely chopped pecans or walnuts

Blend the chutney and cream cheese together by hand or in a food processor. (If using a food processor you won't need to chop the chutney.) Spread the cheese mixture into the groove of each celery stalk. Sprinkle with the chopped nuts.

preceding page: As this early-twentieth-century postcard reveals, Thanksgiving has long been a time for family reunions.

Roquefort Cream Cheese Filling

½ cup Roquefort or other blue cheese, crumbled
1 8-ounce package cream cheese, softened
2 tablespoons milk or cream

Blend the Roquefort, cream cheese, and milk by hand or in a food processor. Spread the cheese mixture into the groove of each celery stalk.

VARIATION Add hot red pepper sauce to taste for a zippy takeoff on Buffalo chicken wings.

Olive and Cream Cheese Filling

1 8-ounce package cream cheese, softened
1 garlic clove, minced
½ cup olives, any type, drained (the liquid reserved) and finely chopped
1 tablespoon reserved olive liquid

Blend the cream cheese, garlic, olives, and olive liquid together. Spread the mixture into the groove of each celery stalk.

OLIVES AND THANKSGIVING

The olives that many of us remember from our childhood relish tray are not the herb-marinated imported olives in vogue today but the ripe, pitted black California olive sold in cans. While olive trees were first brought to California in 1769, the first major planting did not take place until the end of the 1800s. Olives were first canned in California at the beginning of the next century, and mechanical pitting machines came along in 1933. Even today, the vast majority of California's olives end up in a can. Regrettably, there is no documentation for the first time a child stuck an olive on each of his fingers!

HEARTY THANKSGIVING GREETING

Really Easy Cranberry Pecan Brie

No appetizer could be easier than this terrific, warm, and gooey Brie topped with sweet cranberries and nuts. The recipe is much less fussy than the puff pastry–encased Brie that was all the rage in the 1990s. The colorful cranberry topping makes it a pretty addition to the holiday menu.

SERVES 8 TO 10

1 8-ounce round Brie cheese, at room temperature
⅓ cup dried cranberries
1 tablespoon firmly packed brown sugar
1 tablespoon butter
2 tablespoons chopped pecans or walnuts

Make a shallow bowl in the top of the Brie to hold the cranberry topping: Using a paring knife, make a shallow cut in the top of the Brie rind about ¼ inch from the edge. Peel or scrape away the rind in the middle, leaving a ¼-inch rim. Place the Brie on a pretty microwave-safe serving dish and set aside while you make the topping.

Combine the cranberries, brown sugar, butter, and pecans or walnuts in a small microwave-safe bowl. Place the bowl in the microwave and heat on high for 30 to 60 seconds or until the butter melts. Remove the bowl and stir the mixture to combine the topping ingredients. Spoon this mixture on the top of the Brie, place the cheese in the microwave, and heat on high for 45 to 60 seconds. If the Brie is warm, soft, and gooey, it is ready to serve. If it is not, continue to cook in intervals of 15 seconds until the Brie is ready. Serve with plain crackers or French bread.

opposite: An early-twentieth-century postcard, circa 1910.

Seethed Mussels
with Parsley and Vinegar

Seventeenth-century English diners had never heard the word *appetizer,* though they certainly understood the idea of foods served in several large courses for formal or court dinners. For modern diners, however, this lovely period mussel recipe, with its garlic and wine enhancements, makes a perfect first course.

Mussels were considered a "lesser meat" than venison or wildfowl. In spite of this, English cookbooks of the period offer numerous recipes for both "seething" (boiling) and frying mussels. After months of eating a sea diet of dried peas, oats, and salt meats, the passengers on the *Mayflower* were delighted to find mussels when they first made landing on Cape Cod. Many of them ate the mussels they found but soon regretted it: "We found great mussels, and very fat and full of sea-pearl, but we could not eat them, for they made us all sick that did eat, as well sailors as passengers. They caused to cast and scour, but they were soon well again." In 1634, an Englishman wrote, "Muscles [mussels] be in great plenty, left only for the hogs."

Those ringing endorsements aside, other records tell us that mussels were definitely part of the colonists' diet. "Mustles [mussels] there are infinite store...excellent Mustles, to eate for variety, the fish is so fat and large"(Thomas Morton, 1622). They were abundant and easily gathered. It is possible that a dish of mussels was served during the 1621 harvest celebration.

SERVES 8

  4 pounds mussels
  2 tablespoons butter
 ½ cup chopped parsley
 ½ cup red wine vinegar
 ¾ teaspoon salt
 ¼ teaspoon freshly ground black pepper
  2 garlic cloves, minced

Place the mussels in cold water and scrub them clean. Beard them by taking off the tuft of fibers projecting from the shell (if there are any—many farm-raised mussels are beardless). Discard any mussels that are broken or do not close when touched.

Place 1 cup water and the butter, parsley, vinegar, salt, pepper, and garlic in a large pot, cover, and bring to a boil over high heat. Add the mussels and reduce the heat so the mussels cook at a simmer. Cook, shaking the pot occasionally, for 10 minutes or until all of the mussels have opened fully. Keep an eye on the mussels—if cooked too long, they can be chewy. Discard any mussels that have not opened.

To serve, pour the mussels and the broth into bowls. Set an empty bowl on the table for discarded shells.

Sausage-Stuffed Mushrooms

It was not until the middle of the twentieth century that commercially grown white button mushrooms became available in American stores. Before this development, a fear of eating poisonous mushrooms made many people cautious of all fungi. (Less than 5 percent of mushroom species are edible.) Today, white button mushrooms are the most widely available and eaten mushroom in the United States. Happily, many other varieties have also entered the marketplace in recent decades.

This truly fabulous stuffed mushroom recipe is part of the Curtin family Thanksgiving menu. Since he first brought these yummy mushrooms to a Thanksgiving dinner a dozen years ago, Michael Curtin of Goffstown, New Hampshire, has been asked to make them for every family holiday dinner. He was happy to share the recipe in the hope that one of his siblings might take over making them so he can make something else! Mike uses hot Italian sausage and has even been known to add a few dashes of hot red pepper sauce to the stuffing before he fills the mushrooms. This recipe can be assembled a day or two in advance and chilled until you want to bake them. The recipe can also be halved for smaller gatherings.

SERVES 8 TO 10

3 dozen white mushrooms, 2 to 2½ inches in diameter (about 2 pounds)
1 pound Italian sausage, sweet or hot
1 medium onion, finely chopped (about ¾ cup)
4 garlic cloves, minced
4 tablespoons butter, divided
¼ cup finely minced parsley
2 teaspoons dried basil
1 teaspoon dried oregano
1 teaspoon chili powder
½ teaspoon fennel seeds, crushed
½ teaspoon salt
¼ teaspoon freshly ground black pepper
  Pinch of ground cinnamon
¾ cup plain bread crumbs (commercially made bread crumbs are fine for this recipe)
¼ cup grated Romano or Parmesan cheese
4 tablespoons dry cooking sherry

Preheat the oven to 400°F.

Brush any obvious dirt from the mushrooms. Remove the stems and chop enough to make about ½ cup finely chopped mushroom stems. Discard the remaining stems (or reserve for stock).

Remove the sausage from the casings and crumble it into a large frying pan or skillet. Cook over medium heat until the sausage is browned, about 10 minutes, stirring and breaking up the sausage into very small pieces as it cooks. Add the onion and garlic and cook with the sausage until they are softened, about 3 minutes. Add the chopped stems, 2 tablespoons butter, and the parsley, basil, oregano, chili powder, fennel, salt, pepper, and cinnamon. Sauté the mixture for 5 minutes or until the stems are tender. Remove the pan from the heat and stir in the bread crumbs, cheese, and 2 tablespoons of the sherry. Stir to moisten. Taste and adjust seasonings.

Allow the stuffing mixture to cool. When it is cool enough to handle, generously stuff the mushroom caps and place them on a foil-lined cookie sheet. Melt the remaining 2 tablespoons butter and add the remaining 2 tablespoons sherry. Brush the stuffed mushroom caps with the butter and sherry mixture. Place in the oven and bake for 10 minutes, until the mushrooms are tender and the filling is hot. Serve.

Pomegranate and Persimmon Salad

Amelia Saltsman is a Los Angeles food writer, cooking teacher, and television cooking show host. She has special interests in local produce, California food history, and Thanksgiving dinner.

For forty years, Amelia Saltsman's family has celebrated Thanksgiving with an eclectic group of friends. Amelia says, "It's the quintessential California melting pot experience; we all came from someplace else and cobbled together a personal 'traditional' menu.... Besides a glorious roasted bird, our meal always includes a Midwestern corn pudding (my Illinois-bred friend uses recipes from community charitable cookbooks from home), mashed potatoes, gravy, bread stuffing, cranberries, and classic pumpkin pie." Amelia's vegetable side dishes take full advantage of California's abundant autumn produce. In recent years, these side dishes have included kale or chard, "heirloom sprouting broccoli, or sweet end-of-season Blue Lake snap beans. Grilled or roasted butternut squash sometimes stands in for Garnet, Jewel, or Japanese variety sweet potatoes."

This delicious salad, a family favorite, has a permanent place of honor on Amelia's Thanksgiving table. The salad is a wonderful and colorful combination of California produce and Amelia's Middle Eastern heritage. According to Amelia, the salad "evolved from a Waldorf salad my mother used to make (a contribution having absolutely no bearing on our past). Of course, she adapted the classic by adding pomegranate seeds and grapes. Now that I've taken over the fruited-salad job, my mother's been resurrecting her 1960s Jell-O mold recipes."

SERVES 8

- ½ cup walnut or pecan pieces
- 1 ripe pomegranate
- 4 ribs of celery
- 2 small or 1 large fuyu persimmon
- ½ pound mixed baby salad greens
  Extra-virgin olive oil or walnut oil
  Juice of ½ lemon
  Kosher or sea salt
  Freshly ground black pepper
- ½ cup crumbled feta cheese (optional)

Preheat the oven to 350°F. Place the nuts on a baking sheet and toast in the oven until fragrant and lightly browned, 5 to 10 minutes. Start checking after 5 minutes, give the pan a shake to toss the nuts, and return them to the oven until they reach the desired color and aroma. Remember that the nuts will continue to brown a bit after you remove them from the oven, so take care not to overtoast them. If using walnuts, rub off the skins. Pour the toasted nuts into a shallow bowl to cool. Set aside.

To remove the pomegranate seeds: Cut or split open the pomegranate, put the pieces in a bowl of water, and use your fingers to loosen all the seeds. Drain the seeds and reserve.

Use a peeler to pare the strings from the celery. Slice the celery thinly on the diagonal and place in a salad bowl. Cut away the stem from the persimmon. Cut the persimmon vertically into quarters and cut the quarters crosswise into thin slices. Add them to the bowl along with the nuts, greens, and as many pomegranate seeds as you'd like. Drizzle olive oil over salad, squeeze on lemon juice to taste, add salt and pepper, and toss. Sprinkle with crumbled feta cheese if desired.

above: Since 1921, a Thanksgiving Day event memorializing the English colonists (known as "Pilgrim Progress") has taken place in Plymouth, Massachusetts. This photograph is from 1964.

Thanksgiving Cranberry Salad

While packaged flavored gelatins are definitely a late-nineteenth-century development, shimmering congealed "jellies" have been around for centuries. Before the invention of commercial gelatin, housewives made their own gelatin by the labor-intensive process of extracting it from calves' feet. Nineteenth-century cookbook writer Mary Henderson understandably wrote, "I have made calf's feet jelly twice, and never intend to make it again." Molded jellies were fashionable foods eaten mostly by the upper class or reserved for special occasions. All of that changed by the end of the nineteenth century, when commercially prepared gelatin came on the market. Further innovations made it easier and faster to use, and in 1897 the first flavored gelatins (strawberry, raspberry, orange, and lemon) appeared in stores. By the turn of the century, molded gelatin "salads" had become popular in middle-class American families. According to Laura Shapiro's *Perfection Salad,* these tidy salads were heavily promoted by reform-minded domestic scientists, who saw them as a way to make a neat and pretty package out of a mixture of disparate ingredients that would otherwise look sloppy on a plate.

Given the popularity of gelatin dishes, it is no wonder that molded cranberry salads began to appear on many Thanksgiving tables. In recent years, gelatin salads have lost much of their cachet, often featured more for their kitschiness than their glamorous appearance. However, in many parts of the country, particularly the South and Midwest, they are still a necessary and nostalgic part of the holiday menu. This particular recipe has been on Sandy Oliver's Thanksgiving table for years. Brightly colored, it has a nice balance of crunchy and smooth, tart and sweet.

SERVES 6

1 3-ounce package of red gelatin dessert (cherry, cranberry, or raspberry)
¾ cup boiling water
1 16-ounce can of whole-berry cranberry sauce
1 small orange, seeded and chopped or ground with the peel
½ cup chopped peeled apple
½ cup chopped celery
½ cup chopped pecans or other nuts

Oil a 5-cup mold or 6 individual molds. In a medium mixing bowl, dissolve the gelatin dessert in the boiling water. Stir in the cranberry sauce. Chill until the gelatin thickens but does not set. Add the orange, apple, celery, and pecans and mix thoroughly. Pour into the prepared mold. Chill until firm. The salad is ready when it no longer feels sticky on top and the gelatin doesn't move when the mold is tilted.

To serve, chill a serving plate. Moisten fingertips and gently pull the gelatin away from the edges of the mold. Then dip the mold in warm water just to the rim for 15 seconds. Moisten the chilled serving plate with cold water. Center the serving plate on top of the mold and invert, holding the serving plate in place. Shake slightly and then remove the mold carefully. If the gelatin doesn't slip easily from the mold, repeat the process of dipping in the warm water. Position the unmolded salad in the middle of the serving plate. Dry the plate edges.

above: Sons serving in the military during World War II gather around the Fincham family table in Silver Springs, Maryland, 1942.

Golden Glow Gelatin Salad

This classic recipe, one of the most popular gelatin salads, appears frequently in many mid-twentieth-century cookbooks under several names, including Sunshine Salad and the inexplicable Complexion Salad. The 1997 revised edition of *Joy of Cooking* features this salad on the suggested list of dishes for Thanksgiving dinner. A version made with lime gelatin is a must on the Thanksgiving table of many folks in Utah (of course, since their Official State Snack is Jell-O!).

The basic recipe is a citrus-flavored gelatin, a can of crushed pineapple, and grated carrots. Mini marshmallows, cream cheese, and pecans are all popular additions.

SERVES 8 TO 10

 1 20-ounce can of crushed pineapple
 1 6-ounce package (or 2 3-ounce packages) of citrus-flavored gelatin
 2 cups cold water
 4 cups grated carrot

Drain the pineapple, reserving the juice. Place the juice in a large measuring cup and add enough water to make 2 cups liquid. Place the juice and water in a medium pan and bring to a boil.

Place the gelatin dessert in a large heatproof bowl and add the boiling liquid, stirring until the gelatin is dissolved, about 2 minutes. Add the cold water and stir. Refrigerate 1¼ hours or until slightly thickened (to the consistency of unbeaten egg whites). Fold in the pineapple and shredded carrots. Pour the gelatin into an oiled 8-cup mold or bowl. Cover and refrigerate until the gelatin is set, about 3 hours. See the directions for unmolding on page 75.

Curried Pumpkin Bisque

Before the twentieth century, American cooks, particularly those in the North, used pumpkin for pies and vegetable dishes—all part of simple, everyday cooking. In the late twentieth century, however, the humble pumpkin went upscale in a host of new recipes, from risotto to bisques. Vegetable bisques like this one became the rage in the 1970s, and as a glance at the November issue of any food magazine reveals, they have become part of the Thanksgiving tradition. This recipe is smooth and creamy, with a lovely hint of curry. If you want a bisque with more kick for your Thanksgiving starter, dust it with a little cayenne before serving.

SERVES 6 TO 8

- 2 tablespoons butter
- 1 cup diced onion
- 1 cup chopped celery
- 1 cup peeled and chopped carrot
- 2 garlic cloves, minced
- ¾ cup canned crushed tomatoes, with juice
- 4 cups homemade or canned low-sodium chicken or vegetable broth
- 1 15-ounce can pumpkin purée or 2 cups homemade pumpkin purée
- 1 teaspoon curry powder, or to taste
- 2 bay leaves
- 1 cup light cream
- Salt and freshly ground black pepper to taste
- ¼ cup chopped cilantro, for garnish

Melt the butter in a large pot over medium-high heat. Add the onion, celery, carrot, and garlic and sauté until vegetables are very soft, about 10 minutes. Stir in the tomatoes, broth, pumpkin, curry powder, and bay leaves. Bring to a boil. Reduce the heat and simmer the soup for about 15 minutes. Remove and discard the bay leaves. Let the soup cool slightly. Transfer by batches to a food processor or blender and purée until smooth. Return the soup to a cooking pot, stir in the cream, and heat briefly over low heat; do not allow the soup to boil. Season to taste with salt, pepper, and additional curry powder if desired. Serve garnished with chopped cilantro.

OYSTER CENTURY

Oysters were easily the nineteenth century's most popular shellfish—perhaps its favorite seafood, period. Coastal Native People had harvested oysters from very early times, and the colonists arrived with a fondness for them, too. Oysters were so popular that beds along the New England coast were quickly overfished, and oyster cultivation began in the mid-1800s in Cape Cod Bay and Long Island Sound, relying on seed oysters brought from the Chesapeake Bay. Oystermen brought thousands of oysters ashore, where they were packed and shipped inland, even into the West. Oyster saloons sprang up in urban centers, where the hungry lined up to buy raw and roasted oysters and oyster stew. Raw shucked oysters were presented as an appetizer on the most elegant tables, served on special oyster plates that mimicked in china the pearly insides of the oyster shell. Recipes abounded for oyster soup, oyster stew, and oyster sauce, a fashionable accompaniment to fowl, including turkey. Oysters are in season in November, making them a perfect addition to the Thanksgiving table.

above: These military menus include turkey, pumpkin pie, and cigarettes! Thanksgiving Menus, U.S.S. *Case*, U.S.S. *Macon*, 1948, and U.S.S. *Sperry*, 1950.

Oyster Stew

Oysters simply cooked in butter and simmered in rich milk hardly sounds like stew, a word that conjures up potatoes, carrots, and onions. Perhaps we ought to think of it as *oysters stewed,* which, because oysters are delicate, occurs quickly, accounting in part for why oyster stew was, in the 1800s, a kind of fast food sold in restaurants and oyster "saloons."

This recipe is based on one by Fannie Farmer in her *Boston Cooking-School Cookbook.* You will probably not have to heed Farmer's 1896 cautions to pick over and clean the oysters, because of the usual good condition of shucked oysters today. But do reserve the liquor, strain it if you wish, and heat it and the milk separately. Also, be sure to heed Farmer's advice to cook the oysters just until their edges curl; any longer, and the oysters toughen. In her 1854 cookbook, *New Receipts for Cooking,* Eliza Leslie suggests adding a half-pint of cream to the stew just before it is taken off the heat, along with a grating of fresh nutmeg—perfect for a festive occasion like Thanksgiving.

SERVES 8

3 cups milk
¼ cup butter
1 quart shucked oysters and their liquor
1 cup heavy cream
½ teaspoon salt
 Freshly ground black pepper
 Nutmeg (optional)

Warm the milk in a heavy saucepan over low heat until hot but not simmering. Melt the butter in another pan. Add the oysters and their liquor to the melted butter. Heat the oysters until their edges begin to curl or ruffle. Add the hot milk, the cream, salt, and pepper to taste. A few gratings of nutmeg are very good.

THE MAIN EVENT:
Turkey and More

Traditional Roasted Stuffed Turkey and Giblet Gravy

A stuffed turkey, roasted to a golden brown in front of the fire and presented on a china platter with its accompanying giblet gravy in the sauce boat on the side, was the centerpiece of the nineteenth-century Thanksgiving dinner table, as it is today in many homes. Period turkey recipes uniformly call for a roasting time of 10 minutes per pound, while most modern cookbooks recommend allowing 15 to 20 minutes for larger birds. The older cookbooks also remind us of the distinction between roasting and baking in the 1800s: Roasting was cooking before radiant heat from the flames, while baking was cooking in an oven with retained heat. What we call *roasting* today would have been termed *baking* in earlier times, and the nineteenth century is when this changed. In fact, in honor of Thanksgiving, some families in the 1800s dug out the old tin kitchen (a reflective device with a spit) and roasted the turkey in front of a fire, even if they had a cookstove.

This recipe is based on Marian Harland's *Dinner Year-Book,* 1878.

SERVES 12

- 1 12-pound fresh turkey (preferably not self-basting), giblets and neck removed and reserved
- 2 celery stalks, coarsely chopped
- 1 carrot, coarsely chopped
- 1 onion, peeled and quartered
- 1–3 bay leaves
- ¼ cup all-purpose flour
    Salt and freshly ground pepper to taste
- 5–6 cups stuffing of your choice, or see pages 109–119

Place the giblets, neck, celery, carrot, onion, and bay leaves in a medium-sized pot. Cover with water and bring to a simmer while you prepare the turkey.

Set the oven rack in the lowest position. Preheat the oven to 450°F.

Wash the turkey and pat dry with paper towels. Put stuffing in both openings. Follow the directions for stuffing and trussing given in the stuffing recipes. Place the turkey on a sturdy *V*-shaped rack in a roasting pan.

Place the turkey in the oven and decrease the oven temperature to 325°F. Roast the turkey, basting about every half hour. Baste with the giblet broth until there are drippings sufficient for basting in the bottom of the roasting pan. If the breast seems to be browning too rapidly, you may wish to cover it with a piece of foil.

Roast the turkey until a meat thermometer reads 180°F when inserted at the thigh, the drumsticks feel loose when wiggled, and the juices run clear when you poke the bird with a knife. The stuffing temperature should read at least 160°F. For a stuffed 12-pound turkey, the roasting time should be 3 to 3½ hours. Transfer the roasted turkey to a platter or carving board, reserving the pan juices. Allow the turkey to stand for 20 to 30 minutes before carving.

Meanwhile, to make the gravy, pour the pan juices into a large heatproof measuring cup or bowl. Let stand for a few minutes until the fat floats to the top. Remove ¼ cup of the fat from the top of the juices and return it to the roasting pan. Spoon off and discard the remaining fat (or use a gravy separator to pour it off). Add enough of the giblet broth to the pan juices to make 4 cups liquid. If you don't have enough, you can make up the difference with chicken broth or water.

Place the roasting pan with the fat over medium-low heat; you may need to use two burners. Stir in the flour and whisk constantly for 2 minutes; the liquid should bubble gently. Reduce the heat to a simmer and whisk in the broth and drippings mixture (it will spatter, so be careful).

preceding page: This poignant image shows a poor child eating Thanksgiving leftovers at the home of a more fortunate family. *The First Thanksgiving Dinner* by W. S. L. Jewett, from *Harper's Weekly*, November 28, 1868.

Bring to a boil, stirring constantly and scraping the bottom gently to remove the stuck-on bits and to keep the gravy from forming lumps. Add the reserved neck meat and giblets, if desired, and cook for 1 to 2 minutes more, until the gravy thickens. Adjust the seasoning with salt and pepper and serve.

above: By the end of the 1800s, Thanksgiving was well on its way to becoming a celebration of the nation's bounty.

Thoroughly Modern Brined
Roast Turkey with Gravy

Today cooks are confronted with a seemingly endless array of options for preparing the Thanksgiving turkey. Some culinary experts advocate cooking the bird at a high temperature (500°F) for a very short time. Others say the best way to cook a turkey is for a longer time at what may be (by U.S. government standards, anyway) an unsafe 250°F. The debate goes far beyond mere oven temperature; you can cook a turkey breast-side up or down, barbecue it, cook it in a paper bag, deep-fry it, smoke it, brine it, inject it with marinade, cover it with cheesecloth or foil, or even apply ice packs to the breast so the delicate meat is 20 degrees colder than the rest of the bird when it goes into the oven.

This recipe employs several twentieth-century turkey cooking innovations to achieve a moist, flavorful result. The uncooked turkey is brined overnight (you can forgo this step if you use a kosher turkey), a process that keeps the meat moist during the long roasting. The turkey is then cooked for the first 2½ hours breast-side down to protect the delicate breast meat. (If you would rather not turn the bird, cook it breast-side up the whole time and loosely tent the bird with aluminum foil until the last hour of cooking.) Finally, an instant-read meat thermometer is used to monitor the temperature of the bird to determine when it is done.

SERVES 16, WITH GENEROUS LEFTOVERS

2 medium onions, coarsely chopped
2 medium carrots, coarsely chopped
2 celery stalks, coarsely chopped
3 tablespoons chopped fresh parsley, or 1 tablespoon dried
3 tablespoons chopped fresh thyme, or 1 tablespoon dried
2 tablespoons chopped fresh sage, or 2 teaspoons dried
½ teaspoon freshly ground black pepper
½ cup (1 stick) salted butter, melted (or 1 tablespoon butter if you choose to baste the turkey with pan drippings)
¼ cup all-purpose flour
Brined 18- to 20-pound turkey (see page 87), giblets reserved

Place a rack at the lowest level of the oven. Preheat the oven to 325°F.

In a large bowl, mix together the onions, carrots, celery, parsley, thyme, sage, pepper, and 1 tablespoon of the melted butter. Spoon one third of this vegetable mixture into the body and neck cavity of the brined turkey.

Using a thin metal skewer or toothpicks, secure the neck skin to the back of the turkey. Secure the wings to the turkey with kitchen twine or by tucking the wingtips under the back of the bird ("akimbo"). Tie the legs together with a piece of kitchen string. Brush the entire turkey with melted butter.

Grease a large *V*-rack and set it in a large shallow roasting pan (2 to 2½ inches deep). Place the turkey breast-side down on the rack. Scatter a third of the vegetable mixture on the bottom of the pan and add 1½ cups water. Roast the turkey for 2½ hours, basting the back and legs every half hour with butter or pan juices. Add water to the pan as needed during roasting to keep the vegetables moist and prevent burning.

While the turkey is roasting, make a stock for the gravy. Remove and set aside the liver from the packet of giblets. Place the remaining giblets, the neck, and the last third of the vegetable mixture in a large saucepan. (Even if you are not a fan of giblet gravy, use the giblets to flavor the stock; you don't have to add them to the finished gravy.) Add 5 cups water and simmer gently, uncovered, for about 1 hour. If you plan to make giblet gravy, add the liver during the last 5 minutes of cooking time. After the hour of simmering, strain the broth into a bowl, retrieve the neck and giblets if you want to use them in the gravy, and discard the remaining solids. Remove the bits of meat from the neck and chop the giblets very fine. Refrigerate both the broth and the chopped neck and giblet meat until you make the gravy.

When the turkey has been roasting for 2½ hours, remove it from the oven. Using turkey lifters, lift the turkey and turn it breast-side up. (Or, holding a wad of paper towel in each hand, carefully grasp the turkey at each end and turn it breast-side up.) Baste the turkey, return it to the oven, and continue roasting. Basting the turkey every 45 minutes with melted butter or pan juices, roast it until a meat thermometer inserted into the thickest part of the thigh (not touching the bone) registers 175°F to 180°F, about 1½ to 2¼ hours longer. When the turkey is nearly done, if the breast is still pale, raise the oven temperature to 400°F for the last few minutes to brown the skin.

Transfer the turkey to a platter or carving board, reserving the pan juices for the gravy. Allow the turkey to stand for 20 to 30 minutes before carving.

Meanwhile, to make the gravy, pour the pan juices into a large heatproof measuring cup or bowl. Let stand for a few minutes until the fat floats to the top. Remove ¼ cup of the fat from the top of the juices and return it to the roasting pan. Spoon off and discard the remaining fat (or use a gravy separator to pour it off). Add enough of the reserved stock to the pan juices to make

4 cups liquid. If you don't have enough, you can make up the difference with canned chicken broth or water.

Place the roasting pan with the fat over medium-low heat; you may need to use two burners. Stir in the flour, whisking constantly for 2 minutes; the liquid should bubble nicely. Reduce the heat to a simmer and whisk in the reserved stock and drippings mixture (it will spatter, so be careful). Bring to a boil, stirring constantly and scraping the bottom gently to remove the stuck-on bits and to keep the gravy from forming lumps. Add the reserved neck meat and giblets, if desired, and cook for 1 to 2 minutes more until the gravy thickens. Adjust the salt and pepper and serve.

above: A group of young working women gather together to celebrate the Thanksgiving holiday. Note the rather scrawny bird on the left side of the table.

❧ BRINING THE TURKEY ❧

Brining the turkey overnight has been a popular mainstream turkey cooking practice since the 1990s, though the practice of salting meat is hardly new! A few cooking experts are critical of the technique, feeling that brining makes the turkey taste like deli turkey, but most find that brining yields a flavorful and moist bird.

You can get great results with a plain brine, but you can also customize it by adding such ingredients as rosemary, sage, onions, garlic, bay leaves, whole peppercorns, brown sugar, or even chilies. You can also replace part of the water with apple cider or another flavorful liquid. You will need a very large, very clean noncorrosive container. A stainless-steel stockpot or a food-grade plastic 5-gallon container is perfect. You can also use large, heavy-duty food-grade plastic bags. You can double the strength of the bags by putting one inside the other. Note: There is no need to brine a kosher turkey; the koshering process adds the needed salt.

Basic Overnight Brine Solution

1½ cups table salt or 3 cups kosher salt
  2 gallons cold water

Remove the giblets and neck (reserving them for the gravy) and rinse the turkey in cold running water. Pour the salt into your container (or, if you're using plastic bags, mix the solution in a large bowl and then pour it into the bags). Add the water and stir until the salt dissolves. Totally submerge the turkey in the solution and store covered in the refrigerator (or in another location with a temperature between 32°F and 40°F) for 6 to 12 hours. Remove the turkey from the brine and rinse it thoroughly inside and out under cool running water. Pat the skin and both interior cavities with paper towels until dry. Discard the brine. The turkey is now ready to cook.

Roast Turkey with
Indian Spiced Yogurt Marinade

This delicious roast turkey spices up the traditional American holiday menu with familiar Indian flavors and cooking methods. The recipe is adapted from Neelam Batra's wonderful book *Chilis to Chutneys: American Home Cooking with the Flavors of India.* East meets West in this recipe for a turkey marinated overnight in a traditional yogurt spice paste vibrantly flavored with ginger, cilantro, mint, coriander, cumin, garam masala, and paprika. In addition to imparting a wonderful Indian flavor to the classic American bird, the yogurt paste also tenderizes the turkey, keeping it moist and flavorful during roasting. Neelam suggests serving the turkey with your favorite Indian chutney and an assortment of roasted root vegetables.

SERVES 14 TO 16

1	14- to 16-pound turkey, washed, patted dry with paper towels
10–12	large garlic cloves, peeled
1	2-inch piece of fresh ginger, peeled and cut into thin slices
1	cup firmly packed cilantro leaves, soft stems included
½	cup firmly packed fresh mint leaves
1	cup plain nonfat yogurt, whisked until smooth
⅓	cup fresh lemon or lime juice
1	tablespoon ground coriander
1	tablespoon ground cumin
1	tablespoon dried fenugreek leaves
1	tablespoon garam masala (an Indian spice blend)
1½	teaspoons salt, or to taste
2	tablespoons vegetable oil
1	tablespoon paprika
	Shredded lettuce, for garnish

Run your fingers carefully between the skin and flesh of the turkey, starting at the neck opening and moving toward the tail and the thighs, to loosen the skin and create a pocket. Be careful not to tear the skin. Set aside.

In the workbowl of a food processor fitted with the metal *S*-blade and with the motor running, process the garlic and ginger together until minced by adding them through the feed tube. Add the cilantro, mint, yogurt, lemon juice, coriander, cumin, fenugreek, garam masala, and salt and process until the mixture is smooth, stopping the machine to scrape down the sides of the workbowl with the spatula a few times. Remove to a bowl and set aside.

In a small saucepan, heat the oil over moderately high heat until hot but not smoking. Remove from the heat, add the paprika, and immediately stir the seasoned oil into the bowl with the yogurt mixture. (Work quickly, or the paprika will burn.)

Spread about one third of the mixture under the loosened turkey skin and rub another third over the skin and inside the cavity. (Reserve the remaining third in the refrigerator for basting the turkey as it cooks.) Cover the spiced turkey with plastic wrap and refrigerate overnight.

Position a rack at the lowest level of the oven. Preheat the oven to 325°F. Remove the turkey from the refrigerator, fold the wings across the back, and tie them together with heavy kitchen string. Tie the drumsticks together.

Put the turkey breast-side up on a sturdy *V*-rack in a shallow roasting pan (2 to 2½ inches deep). Baste with the reserved marinade and roast, basting every 35 to 45 minutes until the turkey is a rich brown color and a thermometer inserted into the thickest part of the thigh, not touching bone, reads 180°F (3¾ to 4¼ hours). If the skin becomes too brown, loosely tent the turkey with heavy-duty aluminum foil. When the turkey is done, remove it from the oven and allow to stand for 20 to 30 minutes before carving. Transfer to a serving platter, garnish with shredded lettuce, and serve with chutney and root vegetables.

NOTE If you do not have access to an Indian grocery, you can order many Indian food items, including the spices and herbs used in this recipe, through the Ethnic Grocer (www.ethnicgrocer.com) or at Indian Foods Company (www.indianfoodsco.com).

above: Hunting for turkey, the centerpiece of the Thanksgiving dinner, remains a popular holiday activity even today. "Sports in America, Shooting Turkeys for Thanksgiving Day," from the *Illustrated London News,* November 19, 1859.

Pavo Relleno con Moros
Cuban Stuffed Turkey

This Cuban turkey recipe is from Raul Musibay, Glenn Lindgren, and Jorge Castillo, authors of *Three Guys from Miami Cook Cuban*. The three friends are brothers-in-law who "share a passion for good food, good conversation, and a great party." Their fabulous website (www.icuban.com) is dedicated to preserving and promoting Cuban culture, and it features wonderful Cuban recipes.

Glenn Lindgren shared the following information about Thanksgiving in the Florida Cuban community: "Although some highly Americanized Cubans—mostly from Havana's elite—adopted the American Thanksgiving tradition in the forties and fifties, it was not a common celebration in the rest of the country. Most Cubans who immigrated to the United States were introduced to Thanksgiving only after they spent their first November in their adopted country. Today's Cuban Americans celebrate Thanksgiving just like all Americans do. Families gather to eat turkey and have a big feast. However, Cuban exiles in America have done a few things to 'Cubanize' the celebration, bringing their own foods and cooking styles to the Thanksgiving table. This turkey stuffed with black beans and rice is a Miami favorite." Note that in this recipe the turkey is marinated overnight.

SERVES 8 TO 12

1 8- to 12-pound turkey, neck and giblet packet removed

For the marinade

8 garlic cloves mashed with 1 teaspoon salt
1 tablespoon ground cumin
½ teaspoon freshly ground black pepper
1 teaspoon dried oregano
⅓ cup sour orange juice, or ⅓ cup sweet orange juice plus 1 tablespoon white vinegar
⅓ cup olive oil
1 large onion, chopped

For the *moros* (beans and rice)

1½ cups dried black beans
 3 cups long-grain white rice
 6 strips of bacon, chopped
2½ cups diced white onion
2½ cups seeded and chopped green bell pepper
 ¼ cup olive oil
 4 large garlic cloves, minced
 ¼ cup tomato paste
 2 teaspoons ground cumin
1½ teaspoons dried oregano
 1 bay leaf
 3 tablespoons white vinegar
 5 cups chicken stock
 1 teaspoon salt
 ½ teaspoon freshly ground black pepper

For the turkey

 ½ pound bacon, thickly sliced
 ½ cup dry white wine

Wash the turkey thoroughly and pat dry with paper towels.

Mix together the salted garlic, cumin, pepper, oregano, orange juice, oil, and onion and rub the turkey inside and out with the marinade. Place the turkey on a sturdy *V*-rack in a shallow roasting pan (2 to 2½ inches deep), cover, and marinate in the refrigerator overnight.

Cover the dry beans with about 4 cups water in a 2-quart saucepan. Do not add any salt yet. Bring to a boil, and boil for 5 minutes. Remove from the heat and let the beans stand, covered, for 1 hour.

Drain and rinse the beans. Add enough water to cover once again and bring to a boil; reduce heat to low, cover, and cook until tender, 40 to 50 minutes. Drain.

Rinse the rice with cold water until the water runs clear. Set aside.

In a large covered stockpot, sauté the chopped bacon, onion, and green pepper in the olive oil until tender. Add the garlic and sauté for another minute or two. Stir in the tomato paste, black beans, cumin, oregano, bay leaf, and vinegar. Cook for about 5 minutes, stirring gently.

Add the chicken stock and the rinsed rice. Bring to a boil, reduce heat to low, cover, and cook for 30 to 40 minutes, or until the rice is fully cooked. Adjust the seasonings by adding salt and pepper to taste. Remove the bay leaf.

Position a rack on the lowest level of the oven. Preheat the oven to 325°F.

Loosely stuff the turkey cavity with the moros. Tie the legs together and secure the wings to the turkey with kitchen string. Cover the turkey with bacon slices and pour white wine over the top. Place the turkey in the oven and roast until a rich brown color, and a thermometer inserted into the thickest part of the thigh, not touching bone, reads 180°F (3 to 3½ hours). Periodically baste with the pan juices. Remove and discard the bacon during the last 30 minutes to allow the skin to brown.

When the turkey is done, remove it from the oven and allow to stand for 20 minutes before carving.

Stewed Turkey with Herbs and Onions

If you have never thought to boil a turkey, this recipe will make a believer out of you. The sauce, with its spices, onions, and sweet-sour balance of sugar and vinegar, is quite lovely.

This recipe is based on a 1623 recipe from Gervase Markham's *English Housewife* called "To Boil Any Wildfowl." It is easy to imagine a dish like this on a feast table in 1621.

You could use any wildfowl in this recipe. Turkey is in fact not even mentioned in the original, but it is ideally suited to the dish. While the notion of boiling a whole turkey may seem odd, the cooking technique was common into the first few decades of the twentieth century. Boiling was by far the most common method used by American cooks of the past for just about any meat. Boiling required less time, fuel, and attention than roasting; it was economical, resulting in broth as well as cooked meat; and it tenderized tougher or older cuts of meat. While the original recipe calls for a whole bird, the updated recipe is adapted to use with packaged turkey pieces. If you would like to boil a small whole bird (10 to 12 pounds), cut it into 10 pieces first—it is really difficult and potentially dangerous to lift a whole steaming turkey from a pot of boiling broth. For this larger amount of turkey, you will need to double the other ingredients. The original recipe also uses mutton broth. In England in the seventeenth century, mutton was common, so the broth was readily available. In this version, we use the broth from the turkey. Purists can certainly use mutton broth (4 cups) to experience the original recipe as written.

SERVES 6

4 pounds turkey parts (thighs and legs work well for this recipe)
1 teaspoon salt
2 large onions, sliced into ¼-inch rings
  Bundle of fresh herbs, tied (any combination of sage, thyme, parsley, marjoram, and savory), or 2 tablespoons dried
⅓ cup red wine vinegar or cider vinegar
2 tablespoons (¼ stick) salted butter
2 tablespoons sugar
1 teaspoon black peppercorns
¼ teaspoon ground cloves
6–8 1-inch-thick slices of hearty bread, cut in half and toasted or fried until browned

Rinse the turkey pieces and place them in a pot large enough to accommodate them. Cover with cold water and add the salt. Cover the pot and bring the contents to a boil over medium-high heat. Reduce the temperature to keep the broth at a low simmer for 1 hour. Periodically, skim any froth that rises to the surface.

Remove the turkey pieces and set aside to cool. Raise the heat until the broth comes to a boil. Continue boiling, uncovered, until the liquid is reduced by half. This will take about 1 hour.

Add the onions, herbs, vinegar, butter, sugar, peppercorns, and cloves. Simmer for another 20 minutes, or until the onions are soft. While the broth is simmering, cut the cooled turkey into serving pieces.

Before serving, taste the broth and adjust the seasoning. Place the meat in the broth and let it simmer gently for just 1 minute. Pour the turkey and sauce into a serving bowl. Pass the toasted bread slices to serve as a base for the turkey and to sop up the sauce.

above: Meats of every variety are for sale in this illustration of a city market. City dwellers bought their meat for every day and holidays from butcher shops and markets like this. *Washington Market the Day Before Thanksgiving* by W. P. Snyder, from *Harper's Weekly,* November 28, 1885.

The Main Event

Duck with Cranberries and Wine

This is the sort of dish that would have occupied a place of honor on a fine feast table in 1621. The original 1615 recipe uses tart English barberries in the sauce. It is possible that in Plymouth in 1621, English cooks substituted cranberries for the unavailable barberries. The increasing availability of ducks in local grocery stores makes the updated version a lovely option for Thanksgiving.

SERVES 4 TO 6

For the duck

  1 4- to 5-pound duck
2½ teaspoons salt
 10 black peppercorns
  1 medium onion, quartered
     Handful of parsley leaves and stalks
  3 medium onions, halved vertically, then thinly sliced
 ½ teaspoon freshly ground black pepper

For the sauce

  2 cups red wine
 ⅓ cup parsley leaves, minced
  1 teaspoon ground ginger
 ¼ cup dried currants or roughly chopped raisins
2–4 blades of whole mace or ½ teaspoon ground
 ¼ cup cranberries, coarsely chopped
  1 tablespoon sugar
  4 tablespoons (½ stick) chilled unsalted butter, cut into 4 pieces

Rinse the duck inside and out and rinse any giblets included. Place the duck and giblets (except the liver, which can be reserved for another use) in a pot large enough to accommodate them, along with 2 teaspoons of the salt, the peppercorns, the onion quarters, and parsley leaves and stalks. Cover with cold water and bring to a simmer over high heat. Reduce the heat so the broth comes to a very low simmer. Skim off the froth, cover, and simmer for 45 minutes.

Preheat the oven to 400°F. Arrange the sliced onions in a 13 × 9-inch roasting pan. Carefully remove the duck from the broth and reserve the broth. Season the duck inside and out with the remaining ½ teaspoon salt and the ground pepper, and then place it on top of the onions. Roast the duck for 25 minutes, then place it on a carving board and cover loosely with foil.

Meanwhile, make the sauce. Strain 1 cup of the reserved broth and place in a saucepan along with the onions from the roasting pan, the wine, parsley, ginger, currants, and mace. Boil over medium-high heat until the mixture is reduced by two thirds and attains a syrupy consistency.

When the duck has rested for at least 10 minutes, carve it into serving pieces. Place the meat on a heated serving platter and cover loosely with foil.

Add any juices given off during carving to the sauce and stir in the cranberries and sugar. Simmer for another 30 seconds, then remove from the heat. Swirl in the butter, 1 tablespoon at a time, until the sauce is silky. Serve the duck immediately, accompanied by the sauce.

NOTE Simmer the leftover defatted duck broth until it is reduced to one quarter; this makes a very useful stock. Store in the freezer until needed.

1615 Recipe

JOHN MURRELL, *THE NEWE BOOKE OF COOKERY*

To Boil A wilde Duck. Trusse and parboyle it, and then halfe roast it, then carve it and save the gravey: take store of Onyons, Parsley, sliced Ginger, and Pepper: put the gravie into a Pipkin with washt currins, large Mace, Barberryes, a quart of Claret Wine: let all boyle well together, scumme it cleane, put in Butter and Sugar.

Roast Goose

Roast Goose was most certainly eaten during the harvest celebration in 1621. It was celebratory meat in seventeenth-century England and was eaten at Christmastime and on other special occasions. Geese were also associated with Michaelmas, an English holiday on September 29, when tenants often presented their landlords with a goose when they paid their yearly rent. This practice gave rise to the superstition that eating goose at Michaelmas ensures wealth in the coming year. In England, people raised their own fowl or purchased them at markets or fairs. In New England in 1621, there were plenty of wild geese for hunting in the autumn.

Today, frozen and fresh geese are readily available in most supermarkets. While a bit pricey, they are well worth the cost. Goose is all dark meat and has a rich, wonderful flavor that is perfect for special occasions. Although there is a great deal of fat, it is under the skin and not marbled in the meat.

SERVES 8

1 10- to 12-pound goose, fat removed from cavity
$\frac{1}{2}$ teaspoon salt
$\frac{1}{2}$ teaspoon coarsely ground black pepper

Position a rack at the lowest level of the oven. Preheat the oven to 325°F.

Remove the giblets and reserve for another use. Rinse the goose inside and out; pat dry with paper towels. Sprinkle the cavity and skin with salt and pepper. Place the goose on a rack set in a large roasting pan. With the tip of a small knife or a sharp skewer, prick the skin (not the meat) all over. Roast for 90 minutes, and then remove the goose from the oven and carefully spoon most of the fat out of the pan. Return the pan to the oven and continue cooking for 75 minutes more for a 10-pound goose or 90 minutes more for a 12-pound goose.

Transfer the goose to a platter and let rest for 20 minutes before carving. Serve with your favorite chutney or—for a seventeenth-century touch—the mustard sauce on page 144.

above: A Plimoth Plantation re-creation of a colonial housewife busy at her hearth as a goose roasts before a glowing bed of coals.

The Main Event

Chicken Pie

Chicken pies were common nineteenth-century Thanksgiving fare, as the cook could decide how much time she had and gussy up a chicken pie or keep it very simple. Some recipes merely advise the cook to put roast chicken in a pie crust, add gravy, set a crust on top, and bake it. Anyone could do that with the leftovers from a chicken dinner and end up with a perfectly respectable pie. A recipe from Maria Parloa's *Appledore Cookbook* (1880) recommends preparing the chicken as if for a white fricassee before putting the crust on it. Another recipe recommends adding the gizzards, salt, white pepper, nutmeg, mace, and the yolks of hard-boiled eggs, further suggesting that slices of ham or forcemeat balls are a nice addition as well. This modern recipe takes the white fricassee route, but you can gussy up to your heart's content with the ingredients listed above or any cooked vegetables that take your fancy.

SERVES 6

2½–3 pounds chicken pieces
  ¼ cup butter
  ¼ cup all-purpose flour
     Salt and freshly ground black pepper
  1 9-inch pastry crust (or two, if you prefer)

Put the chicken in a large pot. Pour in water until the chicken is barely covered. Bring to a boil over high heat. Reduce the heat and cook at a simmer for 30 to 45 minutes, until the chicken is cooked through and no longer pink against the bone.

Remove the chicken from the broth to cool. Continue to simmer the broth until reduced to about 2 cups. Once the chicken is cool enough to handle, pick the meat off the bones and cut it into bite-sized pieces. Set aside.

Place the butter and flour into a heavy saucepan over medium heat and stir together until the flour bubbles. Add the 2 cups reduced broth gradually, whisking to prevent lumps, and cook until the mixture is thick and smooth, without a floury taste. Add salt and pepper to taste.

Preheat the oven to 425°F.

For a two-crust pie, lay one crust in the bottom of a deep pie plate and arrange the chicken on it. Pour the sauce over the meat. Put on the top crust and crimp closed. If you want a top crust only, arrange the chicken directly in the bottom of the pie plate or baking dish, pour in the gravy, and lay the top crust over, pinching it onto the edges of the pie plate or baking dish.

Bake the pie for 10 minutes, then reduce the temperature to 375°F and bake for 35 minutes more or until the crust is golden brown.

above: In addition to being a time to celebrate the harvest and the domestic realm, Thanksgiving was also a time of homecoming as early as the nineteenth century. From *The Youth's Companion,* November 28, 1895.

Pernil

Puerto Rican Roast Pork Shoulder

For Caribbean Hispanics, roast pork is a favorite celebratory meat for all occasions, and it is commonly served alongside the turkey at Thanksgiving. This delicious roast pork recipe comes from the kitchen of Esther Toro. Mrs. Toro has lived in the Bronx, New York, all her life. Her family's roots are in Puerto Rico, and her Thanksgiving dinner is filled with the wonderful flavors of the Island. In addition to roast pork, Mrs. Toro's Thanksgiving menu includes rice and beans, sweet potatoes, an assortment of pies, and a turkey with a traditional Puerto Rican stuffing of ground meat. The day before she roasts the meats, Mrs. Toro makes a paste of fresh garlic, salt, pepper, oregano, and olive oil and places this mixture under the skin of the turkey and on the pork shoulder to marinate. Mrs. Toro says, "I have had American Thanksgiving and I have had Puerto Rican Thanksgiving, and for me, Puerto Rican Thanksgiving is *much* better!" Our recipe testers seemed to agree—they didn't leave even a scrap of this delicious garlicky roast pork.

SERVES 8 TO 10

1 large head of garlic, broken apart and cloves peeled
   (serious garlic lovers can use 2 heads)
¼ cup fresh oregano leaves or 1½ tablespoons dried
2 teaspoons salt
2 teaspoons black peppercorns
3 tablespoons olive oil
1 5- to 6-pound bone-in pork shoulder, untrimmed

The day before you will serve the roast pork: using a mortar and pestle, food processor, or blender, make a paste of the garlic, oregano, salt, peppercorns, and olive oil.

Place the pork shoulder in a glass or ceramic roasting pan. Using a sharp knife, pierce the pork shoulder on all sides to a depth of ½ inch. Rub the entire shoulder with the garlic mixture, making sure it goes into all of the cuts. Cover with plastic wrap and refrigerate overnight or for at least 8 hours.

The next day, preheat the oven to 450°F.

Place the pan with the pork, fat-side up, on the middle rack of the oven. After 30 minutes, reduce the temperature to 300°F. Cook for an additional 3 to 3½ hours, basting every 30 minutes or so with any pan juices (you can add water to the pan by the half cup if needed). The pork should be tender when pierced with a fork, and the internal temperature of the roast should be 150°F. Remove the pork from the oven and allow to rest 15 to 20 minutes before carving.

❦ OTHER MEATS ON THE THANKSGIVING TABLE ❦

One of the hallmarks of a feast in seventeenth-century England and New England was the presence of several kinds of meat. The menus for the formal dinners of the wealthy might feature more than two dozen kinds of meat. Even middle-class people expected a nice dinner to feature a couple of varieties of meat. Undoubtedly, several meats were served at the 1621 harvest celebration.

For large eighteenth- and nineteenth-century Thanksgiving gatherings, a single turkey hardly sufficed. Other meats filled out the menu—a roast of pork and a substantial chicken pie, for example. In the mid-1800s in Stonington, Connecticut, Grace Denison Wheeler said about her childhood holiday dinner that "the big turkey, brown and shining, [was] accompanied by two big pans of chicken pie and roast pork, crisp and brown, clove studded so it had a spicy odor." Since the holiday fell in the autumn butchering season, it was natural for farm families to have fresh pork on hand. Town-dwellers who purchased their meat from butchers could have fresh meat more easily year-round, and for them a chicken pie required a good deal less work than for the country-dwelling folk, who would have to kill and pluck their own chickens before making a pie.

Tourtière
French Canadian Pork Pie

This French Canadian pork pie is traditionally served after midnight Mass on Christmas Eve, but it is a happy addition to Paul Courchaine's American Thanksgiving table. If you have never tasted tourtière, you are in for a treat—the pie is rich and savory, with a subtle hint of cloves. There are hundreds of family and regional variations of this recipe; a few even skip the pork altogether. Some recipes use potatoes instead of crackers to thicken the mixture, while others add garlic or allspice. Feel free to use the filling to stuff your turkey, as Paul's grandmother (*mémère*) did.

Paul recalls how the tradition started: "Thanksgiving at my French Canadian grandmother's was a large extended family event. She'd begin cooking early in the morning so the turkey and fixings would be ready about midday. She used to stuff the turkey with a meat mixture that really was the traditional filling for the Canadian pies called *tourtière*. After a while, being as practical as most French Canadians, she realized she was leaving a lot of the stuffing stuck inside the bird. So she switched to cooking the stuffing separately. After the midday meal was finished, the table was cleared and the adults began an interminable game of cards, accompanied by shots and beers and language that we youngsters were not intended to hear. At the end of the day, another meal was served. It consisted of slices of leftover turkey in gravy and the same stuffing mix, now made into the traditional pies. It was always accompanied by pickles from the cold cellar part of the house, crispy dills that disappeared quickly from the table."

SERVES 8

- 2 pounds lean ground beef
- ½ pound ground pork
- 1 large onion, finely chopped
- 1½ teaspoons salt
- ½ teaspoon freshly ground black pepper
- ½ teaspoon ground cloves
- 30–36 crushed saltine crackers
- 1 large egg
- 1 tablespoon water
- 1 tablespoon milk
- Pastry for one 9-inch double-crust pie

In a large pot, gently simmer the beef, pork, onion, salt, pepper, and cloves over low heat until the meat is cooked, about 10 minutes. While the meat cooks, move the mixture around, breaking up any chunks of meat—a potato masher works well for this. Transfer the meat and juices to a large bowl. You can leave the mixture as is or, for a finer texture, further mash the mixture with a potato masher. Stir in enough crushed crackers to bind the mixture together. Taste and adjust seasonings to your liking. Let the meat mixture cool.

Preheat the oven to 325°F. Beat the egg with the water and milk to make an egg wash. Spoon the meat mixture into a 9-inch piecrust. Paint the edge of the piecrust with the egg wash. Place the top crust over the meat and trim off any excess dough, leaving a ¾-inch overhang. Fold the edge of the top crust under the edge of the bottom crust. Pinch and crimp the edges to seal. Brush the pastry lightly with the egg wash. Cut several slits in the top of the crust to allow steam to escape. Place the pie on a middle rack of the oven and bake 30 to 35 minutes, or until the crust is golden brown. Slice and serve hot with turkey gravy.

Marinated Roast Venison Tenderloin

Hunting has always been a popular Thanksgiving Day tradition. Native whitetail deer and, of course, wild turkey are favorites of hunters and diners alike. This recipe for a deer tenderloin or saddle roast is from Linda Rago, whose family has lived (and hunted) in the western mountains of Virginia since the 1750s. (Not only does she prepare a wonderful venison roast, but Linda is also an herbalist and the author of several books on traditional Appalachian culture and herbal healing.) Linda's Thanksgiving meal also includes a recipe from her husband's New York Italian family. Since their marriage, the Ragos' holiday meal always begins with a homemade vegetable soup with tiny meatballs (*minestra maritata*), popularly known in America as Italian wedding soup. In Linda's family, it is simply "the soup," and she says it just wouldn't be Thanksgiving without it.

If you are using farm-raised instead of wild venison, reduce the marinating time to 8 hours or overnight.

SERVES 6 TO 8

½–1 cup apple cider vinegar (use the lesser amount for farm-raised venison)
  1 teaspoon peppercorns
  1 onion, sliced
  1 2- to 3-pound venison tenderloin
  2 tablespoons (¼ stick) salted butter

About 24 hours before cooking, combine 1½ cups of water, vinegar, peppercorns, and onion in a glass, stainless-steel, or other nonreactive container large enough to hold the tenderloin. Place the meat in the marinade, cover, and refrigerate for 24 hours, turning the meat 3 or 4 times during that period.

Preheat the oven to 550°F. Remove the meat from the marinade and dry it with a paper towel. Rub the butter over the surface of the tenderloin. Place the meat on a rack in a roasting pan and put in the oven. Reduce the heat to 350°F and cook the tenderloin for 20 minutes per pound or until it registers 140°F on an instant-read meat thermometer. (Venison is too tough if it is cooked beyond the medium-rare stage. The meat will continue to cook as it rests.) Let the venison rest for 10 minutes before carving into thin slices.

above: Wildfowl and venison were two of the foods served in 1621. This is a Plimoth Plantation re-creation of three Plymouth colonists hunting wildfowl in a marsh.

The Main Event

A World of Stuffings

Time-Honored Traditional Bread Stuffing

Some people think the stuffing is the best part of the turkey dinner, and they may be right. This recipe, based on one in Mrs. Elizabeth Ellicott Lea's *Domestic Cookery, Useful Receipts, and Hints to Young Housekeepers* (1853), is for a plain bread stuffing, but feel free to add celery, cooked sausage, boiled chestnuts, sage, garlic, mushrooms, apples, sherry, rosemary, or even the giblets, if you do not want them for gravy. This makes enough stuffing for a 12-pound turkey, but you may wish to double the amount in order to have extra (which you can bake alongside the turkey).

SERVES 6 TO 8

1 pound stale, firm bread
1 medium onion, chopped
6 tablespoons butter
¼ cup chopped parsley
2 teaspoons ground thyme
¾ teaspoon salt (reduce to ½ teaspoon if the broth contains salt)
½ teaspoon freshly ground black pepper
1 large egg, beaten
¼–½ cup hot water or chicken or turkey broth

Remove the crust from the bread, tear the bread into small pieces, and place them in a large bowl. Sauté the onions in the butter until they are soft, and then add them to the bread along with the parsley, thyme, salt, and pepper. Add the egg and toss the bread mixture well, adding enough hot water or broth to make it uniformly moist. The stuffing is now ready for the bird or to be separately baked.

opposite: Children at Boston's North Bennet Street Industrial School, circa 1940. Settlement houses such as this helped immigrants learn about American traditions like Thanksgiving.

Bell's Stuffing

For people across the country with New England roots, stuffing made with Bell's Seasoning is a classic Thanksgiving dish. Bell's Seasoning, one of the oldest American spice mixes, was created by William G. Bell of Newton, Massachusetts, in 1867. The distinctive and earthy blend of rosemary, oregano, sage, ginger, marjoram, thyme, and pepper is an old family recipe that remains unchanged to this day and has only increased in popularity. Bell's Seasoning was an early success story that foreshadowed the changes in food branding that would be fully realized in the twentieth century. A credible argument could be made that the recipe featured on the back of the seasoning box is the best-known and most widely distributed stuffing recipe of the twentieth century.

While New England cooks use Bell's Seasoning throughout the year, the approach of Thanksgiving sends many to the market for a fresh box. These days, far-flung New Englanders in search of the flavor of their childhood Thanksgiving can order Bell's directly from the manufacturer at www.bradyenterprises.com. This recipe was adapted from the recipe on the back of the Bell's Seasoning box.

SERVES 8 TO 12

⅔ cup minced onion
1 cup chopped celery
6 tablespoons butter
16 slices of white bread, cubed and left overnight on a cookie sheet to stale
1½ cups broth, water, or milk
1 tablespoon Bell's Seasoning
Salt and freshly ground black pepper to taste

In a small frying pan, sauté the onion and celery in the butter until softened and golden. Place the bread in a large bowl and add the sautéed vegetables and the broth. Add the Bell's Seasoning, salt, and pepper. Toss until well mixed.

Stuff the mixture into a turkey or bake it separately in a buttered 9 × 13-inch baking dish, sprinkled lightly with additional Bell's Seasoning and baked alongside the turkey for 45 minutes, uncovered, until heated through and nicely crisped on top.

BELL'S®

ALL NATURAL

SALT FREE

THE WILLIAM G. BELL CO.
Since 1867

NET WT. 1 OZ.

SEASONING

Oyster Stuffing

This is an elegant stuffing, one with roots in the plentiful oyster beds of Europe and New England. All the historic recipes caution against breaking the oysters in the stuffing so as to prevent them from disintegrating. Mrs. Henderson's advice in her 1882 recipe to season the stuffing nicely is well taken. You may wish to double the amount so you can bake extra stuffing alongside the turkey. If you are very fond of oysters, use more than are called for in the recipe.

1 recipe Time-Honored Traditional Bread Stuffing (page 109)
1 pint drained, shucked oysters

Make the stuffing according to the recipe instructions. Begin stuffing the turkey, and with each spoonful put in an oyster or two until they are all used up. Be careful not to break the oysters as you put them in.

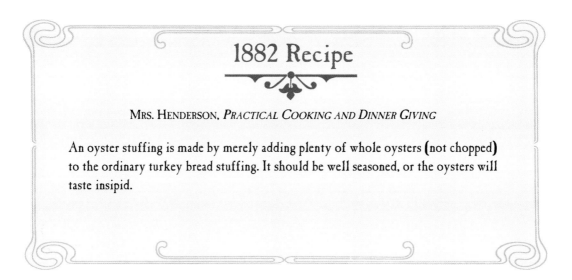

1882 Recipe

MRS. HENDERSON, *PRACTICAL COOKING AND DINNER GIVING*

An oyster stuffing is made by merely adding plenty of whole oysters (not chopped) to the ordinary turkey bread stuffing. It should be well seasoned, or the oysters will taste insipid.

Portuguese Linguiça Stuffing

Large numbers of Portuguese Americans live in southeastern Massachusetts, Rhode Island, New Jersey, Hawaii, and California, and their cuisine is famous for its wonderful seafood recipes, delicious sweet breads, and rich, garlic-infused flavors. This stuffing is a great example, since it is flavored with linguiça, a wonderful garlicky Portuguese pork sausage. Mary Alice Janeiro Post, a renowned cook and the host of a popular Massachusetts television show called *The Portuguese Around Us*, shared this delicious recipe. Mary Alice often adds other special Portuguese dishes to her holiday menu, including loaves of traditional sweet bread, flan for dessert, and a special savory bread made with linguiça and prosciutto (or presunto, a Portuguese cured ham similar to prosciutto).

SERVES 8 TO 10

1 tablespoon olive oil
  Turkey giblets, chopped
1 pound lean ground beef
¾ pound Portuguese linguiça sausage, chopped (see Note)
1 small onion, chopped
1 loaf day-old white bread, sliced, toasted, and broken into pieces
  or cut into 1-inch cubes
1 cup warm milk
¼ cup butter or margarine, melted
  Salt and freshly ground black pepper to taste
  Bell's Seasoning to taste

Heat the olive oil in a large frying pan on medium-high heat. Add the giblets, ground beef, linguiça and onion, and cook until the meat is no longer pink. Place the bread pieces in a bowl and add the milk and melted butter. Add the meat mixture and the seasonings. Mix until the stuffing resembles meatloaf mixture. Stuff in the bird or bake in a 1½-quart casserole at 325°F for 45 minutes.

NOTE Linguiça is available in many grocery stores and specialty markets. You can substitute any other spicy garlic sausage or order from one of several online Portuguese sources, including Alcofa (www.alcofa.com) and Sardinhas (www.sardinhas.com).

Chinese American Rice Dressing

Turkey filled with sweet or glutinous rice stuffing is a Thanksgiving tradition in many Asian American families. This delicious version of a Chinese American rice dressing is from Susie Ling, a California professor of Asian American Studies and a historian at the Chinese Historical Society of Southern California. Susie says this rice dressing is common among families who choose to have a turkey on Thanksgiving. (Some families eat traditional Chinese foods instead.) The sweet rice is cooked with Chinese spices, aromatics, and a variety of other ingredients including Chinese sausage, peas, giblets, mushrooms, and water chestnuts. Many Chinese Americans stuff and steam the turkey, a traditional way of cooking stuffed chickens or ducks. For years, Susie's method has been to cook the dressing in a rice cooker. (She roasts the turkey.) It is also common to buy a roasted marinated turkey from a local Chinese restaurant as one would buy Chinese roast duck or pork.

Susie offers this perspective on Thanksgiving in the Chinese American community: "Thanksgiving for my Chinese American family has certainly evolved. First of all, as immigrants, we did not have a family tradition of Thanksgiving. We don't really like turkey. But Chinese Americans certainly know a lot about big family dinners. So you get the day off, you get married to a 'real' American, the kids are born, and before you know it you are fighting over the pie flavors."

Susie's recipe was inspired by her mother's (which, of course, she makes from memory and has never written down) and "A Chinese American Thanksgiving Turkey" in Ken Hom's *Easy Family Recipes from a Chinese-American Childhood*.

SERVES 8 TO 10

- 1 cup dried black or shiitake mushrooms
- 2 tablespoons peanut oil
- ½ cup minced scallions (white and light green parts)
- 3 garlic cloves, finely minced
- 2 tablespoons peeled, finely chopped ginger
  Giblets from 1 turkey, diced
- 1 pound Chinese pork sausage, diced (see Note)
- ½ pound fresh water chestnuts, peeled and sliced, or 2 8-ounce cans sliced, drained
- 2 teaspoons Asian sesame oil

1   teaspoon salt
½   teaspoon freshly ground black pepper
3   cups glutinous rice, soaked overnight and drained (see Note)
3   tablespoons soy sauce, preferably Chinese
3   cups chicken broth

Soak the mushrooms in warm water for about 20 minutes, until softened. Squeeze to remove any excess water. Cut away and discard the stems and chop the mushroom caps.

Heat the oil in a wok or large frying pan over high heat. Add the scallions, garlic, and ginger. Cook for 30 seconds, stirring constantly. Add the mushrooms, giblets, sausage, water chestnuts, sesame oil, salt, and pepper and continue to stir-fry for a few minutes. Stir in the rice, soy sauce, and broth, mixing well. When the liquid comes to a boil, reduce the heat to low and cover the pot with a tight-fitting lid, or, if you have a rice cooker, place the mixture in the steamer to cook. Cook for 20 minutes, stirring occasionally, until the liquid is absorbed and the rice is tender. Serve alongside the turkey.

NOTE Chinese pork sausage is available at many Asian grocery stores. It can be ordered from Asia Foods (877) 902-0841 or www.asiafoods.com. Glutinous rice, also called sweet or sticky rice, is a short-grained rice that becomes sticky when cooked. It is also available at Asian grocery stores or from Asia Foods. Japanese sushi rice may be substituted, if necessary.

above: This vintage postcard features all the elements of the modern Thanksgiving—Pilgrims, pumpkins, and turkeys.

Southern Corn Bread Dressing

Varieties of corn bread are found in nearly every corner of the country, including some made by Native People since long before Europeans even knew of a land across the Atlantic. That being said, corn bread today is most closely identified with the South and southern cooking. For centuries, corn bread was *the* daily bread of most southerners, particularly slaves, rural folk, and small farmers.

Not surprisingly, corn bread (along with biscuits, another regional favorite) is a typical ingredient in most southern recipes for dressing, including this wonderful version from food journalist Irene Wassell. Irene has prepared her family's Thanksgiving favorite, a recipe from her sister-in-law, for more than fifty years. She says that making the dressing is a family affair and that tasting and tweaking the dressing is a tradition in many southern families, with as many members as are interested swarming in the kitchen to taste and make sure it's perfect. Irene also notes that, due to food safety concerns in the warmer climate, traditional southern cooks rarely stuff the turkey.

SERVES 8 TO 12

- 4 cups crumbled corn bread (recipe follows; see Note)
- 4 cups torn pieces of stale white bread
- 1 teaspoon salt, or to taste
- 1 tablespoon ground sage or 2 tablespoons rubbed
- 4 tablespoons (½ stick) salted butter
- 2 cups chopped onion
- 2 cups chopped celery
- 4 cups chicken broth, homemade or low-sodium canned
- 4 large eggs, beaten

Preheat the oven to 400°F. Butter or spray a 9 × 13-inch baking pan.

In a very large mixing bowl, combine the corn bread and white bread. Add the salt and sage and mix well. Set aside.

Melt the butter in a large skillet. Add the onion and celery and cook about 5 minutes, until the vegetables begin to soften. Add the cooked onions and celery to the bread mixture. Add the broth and stir gently. Taste and add more sage and salt as needed. Stir in the eggs. The mixture will be a little loose.

Pour the dressing into the prepared dish and bake until the top is brown and the dressing is moist but not watery.

NOTE To enhance the taste of the dressing, preheat the oven to 350°F and spread the crumbled corn bread on jelly roll pans (cookie sheets with a lip so the corn bread doesn't slide off). Bake until the bread browns slightly, stirring every 2 minutes or so during baking. Proceed with dressing recipe.

Corn Bread for Dressing

This traditional southern corn bread recipe makes enough for the dressing, with plenty left over for eating right away or freezing for later use.

MAKES ONE 9 × 13-INCH LOAF

    4 cups cornmeal (white cornmeal is used in the South)
    4 teaspoons baking powder
    2 teaspoons salt
2½ cups milk
    4 large eggs, beaten

Preheat the oven to 450°F. Butter or spray a 9 × 13-inch baking dish.

In a large bowl, mix together the cornmeal, baking powder, and salt. Add the milk and eggs and stir until well blended. Pour into the prepared pan and bake 25 to 30 minutes or until the corn bread is nicely browned.

Variations

Like most dressings, this one lends itself beautifully to adaptations. You can add toasted pecans, cooked chestnuts, or raw oysters to the uncooked dressing. If you want to make a version with sausage, sauté ½ pound sausage meat with the onions and celery. For a New Orleans version, reduce the celery and onion to 1½ cups each and add 1½ cups chopped green bell pepper. Cook the vegetables as usual and add 8 ounces cooked andouille sausage to the dressing before you bake it.

Roz Bilahmi

Rice and Meat Stuffing

In 1971, Sama Harp emigrated from Lebanon to Dearborn, Michigan, a suburb of Detroit. Thanksgiving is a favorite holiday for the Harps; Sama loves getting together with her immediate family for the main meal, and then sharing coffee, tea, and dessert later in the day with her extended family and friends.

Sama's menu is a blend of Lebanese dishes and American Thanksgiving foods like turkey and pumpkin pie. She says, "The children expect to see the traditional dishes associated with Thanksgiving, but the adults want the Lebanese-flavored ones." Her menu additions include lentil soup or tomato-vegetable purée soup, leg of lamb, and this meat and rice stuffing decorated with nuts, garlic sauce, and pickled vegetables. Another recent American custom is part of Sama's Thanksgiving as well: "After dinner and since the women did all the cooking, we make the men—my brothers, not the husbands—do the cleaning up. Believe me, this took training from a young age and grew with them."

SERVES 8 TO 10

  2 tablespoons canola or corn oil
  1 pound ground beef or lamb
  2 cups long-grain rice, rinsed and drained
  3 cups chicken, beef, or lamb broth or water
1–2 teaspoons salt (see Note)
  1 teaspoon freshly ground black pepper
  ½ teaspoon ground cinnamon
  ½ teaspoon ground cumin
  ½ teaspoon ground nutmeg
  ¼ cup coarsely chopped canned chestnuts
  ¼ cup blanched and peeled whole almonds
  ¼ cup pine nuts
  ¼ cup shelled pistachios
  ¼ cup golden raisins

Place 1 tablespoon of the oil in a large saucepan over medium heat. Add the ground meat and cook, stirring often, until the meat is brown, about 5 to 7 minutes. Stir in the rice, broth, salt, pepper, cinnamon, cumin, and nutmeg. Reduce the heat to low, cover, and simmer, stirring every 10 minutes or so. Continue to cook the rice, covered, until the water is absorbed and the rice is very tender, about 25 to 30 minutes. During the cooking, add ¼ cup water or more as needed if all the water is absorbed before the rice is done. Taste and add more salt if necessary.

Place the remaining tablespoon of oil in a frying pan over medium heat. Stir in the chestnuts. Then stir in the almonds, pine nuts, and pistachios. Cook and stir for several minutes, until the nuts are lightly browned. Stir in the raisins and remove from heat. To serve, spoon most of the stuffing into a fully cooked turkey with the remainder, garnished with the nut mixture, overflowing onto the serving platter. As an alternative, serve the rice on its own platter, sprinkled with the browned nuts.

NOTE The amount of salt needed will depend on the liquid used. If you use water, add 2 teaspoons salt. If you use broth, start with 1 teaspoon salt. Taste and add more salt if necessary when the dish is finished.

STUFFING OR DRESSING?

According to Damon Lee Fowler in *Classical Southern Cooking*, both *dressing* and *stuffing* are used in the South to describe what is essentially the same food. They are not interchangeable, however. *Dressing* is the term for a bread (or rice) mixture cooked separately from the bird, while *stuffing* is the word for the same mixture used as a filling in roasted meats. Fowler further says that "though the two words are becoming entangled, and one hears a southerner refer to 'stuffing' as 'dressing,' never does one hear it the other way around."

Side Dishes

A Pottage of Indian Corn

Dishes like this one were common fare for seventeenth-century Englishmen in both Old and New England. An English pottage was typically made with meaty broth, oats, and chopped "pot-herbs" boiled into a thick "spoonmeat." In England, everyone from the richest to the poorest ate pottage. In New England, this tradition continued, but the native corn was used in place of the traditional English oats. Pottage was probably served at some point during the harvest meals in 1621; the following spring, an ailing Massasoit asked a colonist to "make him some English pottage, such as he had eaten at Plymouth."

Like our familiar soup recipes, pottages are ideally suited to turning leftover meat or bones into delicious dishes. It is not a great leap to imagine Plymouth colony cooks efficiently and economically converting all of those leftover duck and deer bones into savory pottages to feed the many diners during the several days of the 1621 harvest celebration. If you choose not to feature this dish on your Thanksgiving table, consider making a hearty pottage later with the turkey carcass.

SERVES 6 AS A MAIN DISH, 8 TO 10 AS A SIDE DISH

6 cups broth, with or without leftover meat pieces
2 cups coarse grits (see sidebar, page 123)
1 cup chopped onions or leeks
½ cup chopped parsley
4 cups coarsely chopped spinach, chard, or other leafy green
Salt and freshly ground pepper to taste
Minced fresh herbs (thyme, marjoram, and/or sage) to taste

Bring broth to a boil in a large pot over high heat. Stir in the grits, onions, parsley, spinach, salt, pepper, and herbs; continue until the pottage returns to a boil. Turn the heat to low and simmer uncovered for 10 minutes, stirring frequently. Be sure to stir across the bottom of the pot to keep the grits from sticking.

Remove the pot from the heat and allow to stand covered for about 1 hour, or until the grits are tender. You may need to add more water if the pottage is too thick (it should have the consistency of risotto or thick cooked oatmeal). Adjust seasonings before serving.

1623 Recipe

Gervase Markham, *The English Huswife*

It resteth now that we speak of boild meats and broths, which forasmuch as our Hous-wife is intended to be generall, one that can as well feed the poore as the rich, we will first begin with those ordinarie wholsome boyld-meates, which are of use in every good mans house: therefore to make the best ordinarie Pottage, you shall take a racke of Mutton cut into pieces, or a leg of Mutton cut into pieces; for this meate and these joynts are the best, although any other joynt or any fresh Beefe will likewise make good Pottage: and having washt your meate well, put it into a cleane pot with faire water, and set it on the fire; then take Violet leaves, Succory, Strawberry leaves, Spinage, Langdebeefe, Marigold flowers, Scallions, & a little Parsly, & chop them very small together; then take halfe so much Oat-meale well beaten as there is Hearbs, and mix it with the Hearbs, and chop all very well together: then when the pot is ready to boyle, skum it very wel, and then put in your hearbs, and so let it boyle with a quick fire, stirring the meate oft in the pot, till the meate bee boyld enough, and that the hearbs and water are mixt together without any separation, which will bee after the consumption of more then a third part: then season them with Salt, and serve them up with the meate either with Sippets or without.

Thanksgiving Grits

Food writer Sandra Woodward of Clemson, South Carolina, read an article about the 1621 harvest celebration in *Yankee* magazine that noted the Wampanoag and the English colonists feasted on corn grits. Since then, Sandra has been waging a one-woman campaign to restore grits to the Thanksgiving menu. This is an excerpt of a popular radio essay that Sandra delivered on Thanksgiving Day, 2002, on the topic:

Although I grew up in the South, where my childhood Thanksgiving dinners usually featured stewed hen instead of turkey, for the past 30 years my Thanksgiving menu has been based on the traditional New England model, passed down through my husband's Yankee family for generations. . . . That's why this year, I will be adding a new dish to the menu. This year, along with the stuffed and roasted turkey, the butternut squash, the mashed potatoes, creamed onions, and pumpkin pie, I'll be serving grits. According to no less an authority than the culinary historian at Plimoth Plantation, the "go-to" place for Thanksgiving authenticity, the first Thanksgiving meal most likely featured, and I quote from an article in Yankee *magazine, "dried corn, ground and boiled in water to form a sort of porridge."*

Y'all, it's clear to me that the pilgrims ate grits! *So in honor of their heretofore unnoted place in history, this year I will serve them, too. . . . Who knows? Once the word gets out about their Thanksgiving connection, grits may join turkey and pumpkin as the emblematic foods of this national holiday. You won't believe how good they taste with turkey gravy. It may take a few generations for this "new" tradition to take hold, but I am confident it will. Now that's something to be thankful for!*

SERVES 4

  1 cup stone-ground white grits
3¾ cups water
  1 teaspoon salt
¼ cup half-and-half

Combine the grits, water, and salt in a large heavy-bottomed stockpot. (The heavy bottom is needed to keep the grits from sticking.) Bring to a boil, reduce heat to low, and cover. Simmer 45 minutes, stirring with a wire whisk occasionally to prevent sticking. The grits should be thick, but if they become too thick to stir, add water ¼ cup at a time. When ready to serve, remove from heat, add the half-and-half, and whisk again. Turn off the burner and let the grits stand on the stove for 5 to 10 minutes before serving. Do not allow to boil again once the half-and-half has been added.

Variation

You can also combine the grits and water in a Crock-Pot or other slow cooker and cook them overnight. Check first thing in the morning to make sure the grits are not too watery; if they are, remove the lid and continue cooking to reduce liquid. Add the half-and-half 10 minutes before serving. This makes serving easy and frees up the stovetop for other uses.

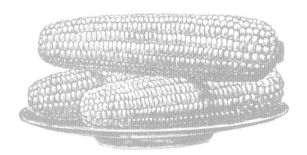

 GRITS OF CORN

While grits are commonly associated with the American South, according to the *Oxford English Dictionary* the word was in use in sixteenth-century England. The English who traveled to the New World in the seventeenth century referred to the coarser pieces of any grain—but usually oats—as *grits,* a dialect form of *groats.* The corn recipes in this book call for coarse grits of flint corn (sometimes called *samp* in modern markets). Finely ground grits used for Southern grits just will not do. Coarse white grits, sold under the brand name Gonsalves (a Portuguese food company), are available at many gourmet stores and large supermarkets. You can also order coarse white grits from Plimoth Plantation at www.plimoth.com.

Stewed Pumpkin
"The Ancient New England Standing Dish"

New World pumpkins and squashes were introduced in Europe in the late fifteenth century. By the time the colonists made their way to Plymouth, "pompions" had gained widespread acceptance in England. In New England, stewed pumpkin was common, everyday fare—a "standing dish"—particularly in the fall and winter. The lyrics to a song, traditionally dated 1630, reveal the colonists' dependence on pumpkins:

> *For pottage, and puddings, and custards, and pies,*
> *Our pumpkins, and parsnips are common supplies;*
> *We have pumpkin at morning and pumpkin at noon,*
> *If it was not for pumpkin we should be undone.*

Edward Johnson, who came to Boston in 1630, wrote, "Let no man make a jest at Pumpkins, for with this fruit the Lord was pleased to feed his people to their good content, till Corne and Cattell were increased." Perhaps this passage was in response to the merry lyrics of the song.

Pumpkin was undoubtedly served in 1621 at the harvest celebration. This recipe for stewed pumpkin is an updated version of one of the earliest written recipes from New England. John Josselyn, an early traveler to New England, recorded it and his description of the common dish is full of wonderful details that provide both a sense of how the finished dish should taste ("tart like an apple") and a vivid glimpse into a colonial kitchen ("stew them upon a gentle fire a whole day").

SERVES 8

4 cups cooked and mashed pumpkin or other squash
4 tablespoons butter
1–2 tablespoons cider vinegar
1–2 teaspoons ground ginger (or any combination of nutmeg, cloves, cinnamon, and pepper, to taste)
1 teaspoon salt

Place the pumpkin, butter, vinegar, ginger, and salt in a saucepan over low heat. Stir and heat until all of the ingredients are well combined and hot. Adjust the seasonings to your liking and serve.

above: Pumpkin appeared regularly on colonial tables and was likely served at the 1621 harvest celebration, as shown in this Plimoth Plantation re-creation.

1672 Recipe

JOHN JOSSELYN, *NEW-ENGLANDS RARITIES DISCOVERED*

The Ancient New England standing dish:

The Housewives manner is to slice [the Pompions] when ripe, and cut them into dice, and so fill a pot with them of two or three Gallons, and stew them upon a gentle fire a whole day, and as they sink, they fill again with fresh Pompions, not putting any liquor to them; and when it is stew'd enough, it will look like bak'd Apples; this they Dish, putting Butter to it, and a little Vinegar, (with some Spice, as Ginger, &c.) which makes it tart like an Apple, and so serve it up to be eaten with Fish or Flesh: It provokes Urin extreamly and is very windy.

A Boiled "Sallet" of Spinach

In the fall of 1621, a number of "herbs" were available in English colonial gardens, including carrots, parsnips, parsley, cabbage, turnips, fennel, chard (called *beets* in the period), leeks, spinach, thyme, marjoram, hyssop, and sage. Onions, already harvested and stored, were also available for use in cooking. Late-summer plantings may have yielded lettuce, endive, and spinach.

Spinach was a popular ingredient in period recipes for everything from tarts to boiled "sallets" (salads) like the one below. Raw salads were popular among the English upper class in the seventeenth century, but the middle and lower classes (and many physicians) tended to be wary of raw vegetables and fruits. However, little that came out of the gardens at Plymouth escaped the cook pot. Many vegetables were simply boiled and buttered or dressed with a bit of olive oil (which was actually the most commonly used oil then). This recipe, with its sauce of butter, vinegar, sugar, and currants, is a slightly fancier but still common preparation.

SERVES 6

- 3 pounds fresh spinach, well washed, stemmed, and chopped (do not dry)
- 3 tablespoons butter
- 1/3 cup dried currants or raisins
- 2 tablespoons cider vinegar or red wine vinegar
- 1–2 tablespoons sugar
- Salt to taste

Pile the washed spinach in a large pot over medium heat, moving it about until it is wilted and considerably reduced in volume, 3 to 5 minutes. Press the spinach against the side of the pot, then drain off any excess water from the bottom, and add the butter, currants, vinegar, sugar, and salt. Continue cooking briefly, tossing the spinach to coat it with the sauce. Using a slotted spoon, transfer to a bowl to serve.

opposite: Historians learn about how people cooked and ate in the seventeenth century from paintings like this one. Detail, *Family Scene,* oil on panel, 1575–1600, after Martin van Cleve.

1623 Recipe

GERVASE MARKHAM, *THE ENGLISH HUSWIFE*

To make an excellent compound boild Sallat: take of Spinage well washt, two or three handfulls, And put it into faire water, and boile it till it bee exceeding soft, and tender as pap: then put it into a Cullander and draine the water from it, which done, with the backside of your Chopping knife chop it, and bruise it as small as may be: then put it into a Pipkin with a good lump of sweete butter, and boile it over againe: then take a good handfull of Currants cleane washt, and put to it, and stirre them well together; then put to as much Vinegar as will make it reasonable tart, and then with Suger season it according to the taste of the Master of the house, and so serve it upon sippets.

Mashed Potatoes and Turnips

This recipe will give you a great new spin on that Thanksgiving classic, mashed potatoes. It is based on a recipe by Mrs. E. A. Howland of Worcester, Massachusetts, published in *The New England Economical Housekeeper* (1845). In it, she called for mealy potatoes, referring to those with a pleasantly dry flesh; a russet type is better for mashing than the waxier reds. You may use either the small purple-topped turnips or the larger, yellow, and more flavorful rutabagas.

The phrase *turnip sauce,* as used by Mrs. Howland, is a particularly American term for a side dish of vegetables. Garden sauce, or "sass," as it was sometimes called, indicated an accompaniment to meat, not literally a pourable sauce. The term reveals one early American attitude toward vegetables. The most important part of the meal was the meat. Bread or grain-based pudding, the starchy part of the meal, was next most important. Vegetables were merely the "sauce." But by the time Mrs. Howland wrote her recipe, potatoes were assuming prominence at the table. In fact, in some households, potatoes were already indispensable at the main meal of the day, and certainly at Thanksgiving.

SERVES 10 TO 12

3   pounds turnips
3   pounds floury potatoes such as russets
1   cup light cream
    Salt and freshly ground pepper to taste

Peel and cut the turnips and potatoes into 1- or 2-inch chunks. Boil separately until tender. Drain. While they are still hot, mash them and blend them together, adding the cream, salt, and pepper.

Creamed Onions

Based on the 1853 recipe from Mrs. Elizabeth Ellicott Lea, in *Domestic Cookery, Useful Receipts, and Hints to Young Housekeepers,* these creamed onions are rich, buttery, and tender. Modern recipes are direct descendants of the nineteenth-century onions boiled in milk or served with cream, butter, salt, and pepper. Serving cooked onions so the diners would not reek after the meal was a sure sign of gentility. Creamed onion recipes grew more elaborate as the century progressed. In the early decades of the nineteenth century, cooks simply boiled onions in milk and served them with salt and pepper. Later, more complicated recipes advised pouring off the milk and adding cream and butter. At the end of the century, the cooked onions were dressed with a separately made cream or white sauce.

White sauce may seem a little trite today, perhaps because too many are based on gluey packaged mixes, but this recipe uses real cream and is not thickened with flour, so it is very flavorful. A modern cook can add curry powder to cream sauce, or at the very least grate nutmeg into it, to make a delicious dish out of simple boiled onions. If you start with fresh pearl onions, make peeling easier by boiling them unpeeled for a minute or so. Then you can cut the ends off and just squeeze them out of their skins.

SERVES 6 TO 8

2 pounds small or pearl onions
1 cup milk
1 cup water
1 cup cream
2–3 tablespoons butter
    Salt and pepper to taste
    A grating of nutmeg (optional)

Boil the unpeeled onions for 1 to 2 minutes. Remove the onions from the water, cut the ends off, and slip off the skins. Cook the peeled onions in a saucepan with the water and milk until tender. Drain, add the cream, butter, and salt and pepper, and return to low heat until the cream is heated through. If you wish, grate a little fresh nutmeg over the top.

Finnish Turnip Casserole

This recipe came to America with Joanne Ciesluk's Finnish grandmother, Tyyne Justina Holm Maki, who immigrated in 1912 to Salt Lake City, Utah. The family later relocated to Massachusetts, where Joanne lives today. For her family, it would not be Thanksgiving without this delicious recipe, which even professed non-turnip-eaters enjoy. The rest of the family holiday meal includes fruit cup, turkey with herb and giblet dressing, mashed potatoes, gravy, French green beans with almonds, creamed onions, cranberry sauce, cranberry relish, hot rolls, and squash pie.

SERVES 8

1 large (about 3½ pounds) rutabaga
2 teaspoons salt
1 large egg, beaten
½ cup milk
¼ teaspoon nutmeg, preferably freshly grated
¼ teaspoon freshly ground black pepper
¼–⅓ cup sugar, depending on taste
⅓ cup plain bread crumbs
2 tablespoons butter, melted

Cut the rutabaga into large chunks and cut off the peel to remove the waxy coating. Further cut the rutabaga into chunks or strips of roughly the same size. Place the pieces in a large saucepan and add enough boiling water to cover. Add 1½ teaspoon of the salt, cover the pan, and boil for 20 to 30 minutes, until tender. Drain the rutabaga and mash using a potato masher. Allow the rutabaga to cool.

Preheat the oven to 350°F. Butter or spray an 8½ × 4½ × 2 ½-inch loaf pan or a 1 ½-quart casserole.

Mix the mashed rutabaga with the remaining ½ teaspoon salt, egg, milk, nutmeg, pepper, and sugar, and stir until the mixture is smooth. Spread in the prepared pan. Mix the bread crumbs with the melted butter and sprinkle them over the top of the rutabaga mixture.

Bake 35 minutes, until it is hot and the top nicely browned. Serve hot.

Deluxe Sweet Potato Casserole
with Marshmallows

Twentieth-century American cookbooks offer numerous recipes for sweetened sliced or mashed sweet potatoes. (Northern writers often identified these recipes as "southern dishes.") It was not until 1929, according to Jean Anderson in *The American Century Cookbook,* that marshmallow topping for the sweet potato casserole first appeared in print—specifically, in Ida C. Bailey's *Vital Vegetables.* For many Americans, this dish, marshmallows and all, is a must-have on the holiday table. This version is adapted from the 1930 edition of Fannie Farmer's *Boston Cooking-School Cookbook.*

SERVES 10 TO 12

6 medium sweet potatoes (3½–4 pounds), scrubbed
3 tablespoons salted butter, at room temperature
½ teaspoon salt
½ teaspoon ground cinnamon
¼ teaspoon ground nutmeg, preferably freshly ground
¼ teaspoon ground allspice
¼–½ cup milk or orange juice, as needed
½ cup drained chopped pineapple (optional)
½ cup chopped pecans (optional)
Marshmallows to cover the casserole (about 25)

Place the whole unpeeled sweet potatoes in a large saucepan. Cover with cold water, bring to a boil over high heat, reduce the heat to medium-high, and simmer until the potatoes are tender, 30 to 40 minutes, depending on the type and shape of the potatoes. Drain and allow the potatoes to cool.

Preheat the oven to 375°F. Butter or spray a 3-quart baking dish. When the sweet potatoes are cool enough to handle, peel and mash or rice them. Add the butter, salt, cinnamon, nutmeg, and allspice. Stir in enough milk to make the mixture light and creamy. Stir in the pineapple and pecans. Spoon the mixture into the prepared baking dish. Press the marshmallows into the surface of the potato mixture. Bake for 30 to 40 minutes, or until the sweet potatoes are heated through and the marshmallows are a lovely brown color.

MARSHMALLOWS

Marshmallow is the name of both a plant and a type of confection. In fact, the confection took its name from the plant, which originally contributed an essential ingredient to it. Confections made from the marshmallow plant have been made for thousands of years, the earliest recipes dating to ancient Egypt.

The modern marshmallow candy was developed in the early 1800s, and by the end of the century other thickeners had replaced the marshmallow root. Modern marshmallows are made from sugar syrup cooked to the hardball stage, combined with gelatin or gum Arabic, and whisked into beaten egg whites. The mixture is dusted with powdered sugar and cut into cubes or rounds. Of course, most people no longer make their own marshmallows. In fact, according to the folks at Jet-Puffed Marshmallows, Americans purchase a truly mind-boggling 90 million pounds of commercially made marshmallows each year.

Candied Sweet Potatoes

This wonderful California take on the standard candied sweet potato dish is from *Helen Brown's West Coast Cookbook* (1952). The book is now more than fifty years old but, a true classic, it has withstood the test of time. The recipes are just as fresh and relevant today as they were when they were new.

A survey of twentieth-century cookbooks reveals a number of interesting variations on this Southern classic. Alternative sweeteners for the syrup base include sugar, molasses, cane syrup, corn syrup, and even maple syrup (in a Vermont cookbook, of course!). Almonds, pecans, raisins, or currants may also be added. The combination of honey and orange in this recipe provides a nice, bright flavor.

SERVES 6 TO 8

2 pounds sweet potatoes, peeled and cut into ¼-inch slices (about 5 cups)
1 cup orange juice
¼ cup honey
¼ cup (½ stick) salted butter, melted
¼ teaspoon salt
1 tablespoon slivered orange peel (see Note)

Preheat the oven to 350°F.

Arrange the sweet potato slices in a 1½-quart flameproof baking dish. Combine the orange juice, honey, butter, salt, and orange peel. Pour this mixture over the sweet potatoes.

Cover and bake for 15 minutes. Uncover and baste with the sauce. Continue to cook uncovered, basting once or twice, for 25 minutes, or until the potatoes are tender. Set the oven to broil and place the baking dish under the broiler until the tops of the slices are lightly browned, about 5 minutes. Watch carefully to avoid burning the potatoes!

NOTE To make the slivered peel, peel the zest (the thin colored outside layer of a citrus fruit) from an orange and slice it into very thin slivers.

"*I love the way you make those yams. You'll have to give me the recipe before your culture is obliterated from the face of the earth.*"

Green Bean Casserole

In order to make a "real" Thanksgiving, certain dishes must be present on the table. These necessary dishes vary from person to person, but for more than 20 million Americans, this green bean casserole is one of them.

The recipe, which uses canned soup, was created in 1955 by Campbell Soup's staff of home economists, and it has been Campbell's most requested recipe ever since. French's Fried Onions, the canned topping for this dish, had been available since 1933, but sales didn't really take off until they were made famous as an ingredient and topping for the recipe. According to French's, 50 percent of their Fried Onions sales occur at Thanksgiving, Christmas, and Easter. In the 1950s, when this casserole was invented, it was called a *jiffy casserole* because it involved minimal preparation and cleanup.

SERVES 8

1 10¾-ounce can condensed cream of mushroom soup
½ cup milk
1 teaspoon soy sauce or Worcestershire sauce
⅛ teaspoon freshly ground black pepper
2 16-ounce cans French-cut green beans, drained, or 2 16-ounce packages frozen French-cut green beans, cooked and drained
1 2.8-ounce can French's Fried Onions

Preheat oven to 350°F.

In a medium bowl, whisk the condensed soup, milk, soy sauce, and pepper until smooth. Stir in the beans and half of the onions. Pour the mixture into a 1½-quart casserole. Bake for 25 minutes, uncovered, until the mixture is hot and bubbling. Stir well, top with the remaining onions, and bake for 5 minutes more, or until the onion topping is nicely browned.

Brussels Sprouts with Chestnuts

Brussels sprouts and chestnuts are both fall crops, making them a perfect combination for Thanksgiving. (And though Brussels sprouts are now available year-round, they are at their best in the late fall.) Compared with their cousins, cabbage and kale, Brussels sprouts are a relatively new vegetable in American gardens. Thomas Jefferson planted some in 1812, but they did not become common fare until the turn of the twentieth century. Their popularity increased—as a frozen vegetable—with the development of the frozen food industry in the 1940s.

Few vegetables are as maligned as Brussels sprouts. If you are among those traumatized early on by the mushy, odiferous school cafeteria version, it is time to give Brussels sprouts another try—fresh ones are nutty and sweet. They are shown to their best advantage in this classic recipe.

SERVES 6

2 pints (1½ pounds) Brussels sprouts, the smallest you can find
4 tablespoons (½ stick) salted butter
1 10-ounce can whole chestnuts, drained
  Salt and freshly ground black pepper to taste
2 tablespoons chopped fresh parsley
½ teaspoon ground cumin or a few gratings of fresh nutmeg (optional)

Trim the Brussels sprouts by cutting a small slice from the stem end and removing any leaves that are discolored or dry. Wash the sprouts in fresh cold water. Cut an *X* in the bottom of the stem end (an old-fashioned technique that helps ensure even cooking) and steam or boil the sprouts until just tender, anywhere from 5 to 12 minutes, depending on their size. In a mixed-sized batch, you can cook the larger sprouts for about 6 minutes and then add the smaller ones to the pot. When the sprouts are cooked, drain them and set aside. Melt the butter in a large skillet or saucepan over medium heat. Add the chestnuts and Brussels sprouts. Season to taste with salt and pepper. Cook for 3 to 5 minutes, until the vegetables are heated through. Add the parsley and the cumin or nutmeg and serve.

Creamy Green Bean and Mushroom Casserole

This is our own healthier take on the green bean casserole. The recipe uses fresh beans and lots of mushrooms in a classic white sauce. This version has considerably less sodium than the casserole made with canned soup, and it tastes wonderful. On the down side, our homemade version uses more pots and pans than the "jiffy" recipe.

SERVES 8

- 2 pounds fresh green beans
- 1½ teaspoons salt
- 6 tablespoons (¾ stick) salted butter
- ¼ cup minced onion
- 2 garlic cloves, minced
- 1 pound white or cremini mushrooms, cleaned, trimmed, and sliced
- 3 tablespoons all-purpose flour
- 1½ cups milk
- ¼ teaspoon freshly ground black pepper
- ⅛ teaspoon fresh grated or ground nutmeg
- 2–4 dashes Tabasco sauce, or to taste
- ½ cup plain dried bread crumbs

Preheat the oven to 350°F.

Trim and cut the green beans into 1- to 2-inch lengths. Place them in a medium saucepan, add 1 teaspoon of the salt, and cover with water. Set over high heat until the water boils, then reduce to a simmer, cover, and cook until the beans are tender, 10 to 15 minutes. Drain well and set aside.

Melt 2 tablespoons of the butter in a medium sauté pan set over medium heat. Add the onion and cook, stirring occasionally, until the onion is tender and translucent, 3 to 5 minutes. Add the garlic and mushrooms and sauté until the mushrooms are soft and most of the mushroom liquid is cooked off, about 10 minutes. Remove from the heat and set aside.

In a large saucepan, melt 2 tablespoons of the butter over low heat. Whisk in the flour and cook, stirring frequently, 3 or 4 minutes. Add the milk, whisking constantly to prevent lumps. Cook over low heat until nicely thickened, 3 to 5 minutes. Add the remaining ½ teaspoon salt, pepper, nutmeg, and Tabasco. Taste and adjust the seasonings. Remove the saucepan from the heat and stir in the green beans and the mushroom mixture. Spoon into a 2-quart casserole.

Melt the remaining 2 tablespoons butter and stir in the bread crumbs. Spread the bread crumb mixture over the casserole. Bake uncovered for about 30 minutes, until the bread crumbs are nicely browned and the sauce is bubbling.

above: In the twentieth century, annual Thanksgiving pageants took place in schools across the country. These events celebrated the "First Thanksgiving" without depicting the perspectives of the Wampanoag and other Native People. North School Thanksgiving Pageant, circa 1920, Portland, Maine.

Corn Pudding

Not surprisingly, corn, a plant native to the Americas, is popular at Thanksgiving in everything from a modern version of the Native dish succotash to southwestern-flavored turkey dressings with corn and jalapeños. In the South and Midwest, custardy corn puddings are popular Thanksgiving side dishes. In the summertime, corn pudding recipes are often made with fresh corn. This version made with canned corn is a tasty fall and winter variation.

This recipe is from Lee and Kitty Pritty of Virginia's Northern Neck. Their Thanksgiving menu includes turkey and a cured Virginia country ham, a common southern addition to Thanksgiving. The side dish is on the sweet side—the perfect complement to a country ham. Other family favorites include fried oysters, collard greens, sweet potatoes with marshmallows, canned cranberry sauce, macaroni and cheese (for the children), "congealed salad" (made with 7-Up, fruit cocktail, pineapple, and lime gelatin), assorted rolls spread with molasses, and a variety of homemade pickles, including spiced peaches. The desserts typically include sweet potato pie, pumpkin pie, chocolate pie, brownies, rum cake, coconut cake, and red velvet cake. Sweet tea (iced) always accompanies the meal.

SERVES 4 TO 6

2 tablespoons all-purpose flour
1 cup milk
2 large eggs, beaten
1 tablespoon sugar
1 17-ounce can creamed corn
2 tablespoons butter, melted
½ teaspoon vanilla extract

Preheat oven to 350°F.

Stir the flour into ¼ cup of the milk, making sure no lumps of flour are left. (You can also put the mixture through a mesh strainer to get rid of lumps.) Combine this paste with the eggs, sugar, corn, butter, and vanilla in a medium bowl. Pour into a buttered 8 × 8-inch pan or 1-quart casserole. Bake until set in the middle, 30 to 40 minutes. The pudding will be custard-like when done; a table knife inserted into the pudding should come out clean. Serve hot.

Pennsylvania German Sauerkraut

Sauerkraut is a traditional Thanksgiving dish for Americans of German heritage, and in places where they settled, like Baltimore, Maryland, it is commonly served alongside the turkey. This particular recipe is from Ellen Hazen, who now lives in Massachusetts. Like many Americans, her Thanksgiving is a patchwork of recipes from family members. The sauerkraut is from her Pennsylvania German mother. As for the rest of the menu, Ellen says: "We have ended up with *a lot* of food 'musts' in addition to the sauerkraut: 'likkered turkey' (made with wine) with mushroom stuffing, gravy, mashed white potatoes, mashed sweet potatoes, Dutch candied rutabagas, broccoli with herb butter, peas and onions, relish tray, pumpkin pie, mince pie with my grandmother's hard sauce. It just goes on and on. If we get a new family member, we're going to have to negotiate a food tradition swap, or we'll need to get a bigger table!"

Ellen says the dish tastes even better if made several days ahead.

SERVES 8

- 1 large onion, chopped
- 2 tablespoons bacon drippings
- 1 quart (2 pounds) fresh sauerkraut, drained (found in bags in the dairy case of most markets), or canned or jarred sauerkraut
- 1 Granny Smith apple, peeled and grated
- 1 tablespoon light brown sugar
- 1 teaspoon caraway seeds

In a large frying pan, sauté the onions in the bacon drippings until softened. Add the drained sauerkraut and grated apple and mix well.

Cover the sauerkraut mixture with water; add the brown sugar and caraway seeds. Cook uncovered for about 30 minutes. Continue cooking for about another 30 minutes, adding small amounts of water if the pan looks dry. The sauerkraut should be thick and juicy, but not runny.

above: Norwegian emigrants beginning their journey to America. Large numbers of Norwegians began arriving in the first half of the 1800s.

Norwegian Lefsa Bread

Lefsa, a traditional Norwegian soft, flat potato bread, has been part of Eric Sterbenk's Thanksgiving for as long as he can remember. This recipe is from Eric's grandmother, Minnie Schumacher. Eric remembers "Grandma baking it on the wood cookstove in the kitchen, and it was wonderful." On the occasions when he couldn't go home for the holiday, a shipment of homemade lefsa would arrive in the mail from Wisconsin. Eric's experience is not unique; in Norwegian American families, lefsa is as much a part of the holiday as the turkey.

For a recipe with such a short list of ingredients, there is an astounding number of family lefsa variations and techniques. But there does seem to be nearly universal agreement about how to eat lefsa: The tender, warm lefsa are spread with butter, sprinkled with sugar or cinnamon sugar, and rolled up.

MAKES ABOUT 12 LEFSA

5 large russet potatoes
1 teaspoon salt
3 tablespoons butter or lard
½ cup flour to each cup of mashed potatoes

Peel the potatoes and place them in a large pot. Cover with cold water. Bring to a boil and let the potatoes cook until soft but not mushy, about 20 to 30 minutes. Drain and mash or rice the potatoes. While the potatoes are still hot, add the salt and butter. Let cool. (Some cooks let the potatoes cool overnight in the refrigerator or on a cool porch.)

Measure the volume of mashed potatoes and add the appropriate amount of flour, blending with a fork. Work the dough into a ball, but do not knead it. Divide the dough in half and place one half in the refrigerator while you work with the other. Roll the dough into a log and cut off a piece about the size of a walnut. Roll out using a lightweight floured rolling pin on a lightly floured surface. Make the lefsa as thin as possible. Bake the lefsa on a griddle or an electric frying pan on medium heat (about 350°F). Cook one side until lightly speckled with brown spots, and then turn. When baked, place the lefsa on a clean dishtowel and fold it over to keep the bread warm and prevent it from becoming dry.

Sauces and Condiments

Mustard Sauce

Mustard was without a doubt the most common condiment in the seventeenth century. It was served with every sort of meat and was thought to be especially good with goose, brawn (pickled pork), and fish. In England, mustard was often made at home quite simply by grinding mustard seed and adding vinegar. Finer mustards could also be purchased from commercial mustard makers. Tewksbury mustard, which included horseradish, was especially well liked.

Mustard seed came across the Atlantic with the colonists. It was included on colonial supply lists and was a common condiment on ship as well as on land. Sharp and pungent, mustard was not a food well liked by the Native People. In 1602, explorer Bartholomew Gosnold shared some food with Native men and recorded that they "misliked nothing but our mustard, wherat they made many a sowre face."

This sauce is based on a 1669 recipe from Sir Kenelme Digbie's *The Closet Opened.*

MAKES 2 CUPS

  1 cup yellow mustard seeds
  3 tablespoons sugar
1½ teaspoons salt
 ½ teaspoon freshly ground pepper
  2 teaspoons ground ginger
  2 cups red wine vinegar or cider vinegar

Grind the mustard seed in a spice grinder, blender, or mortar and pestle to the texture of coarse cornmeal. Place the mustard in a medium bowl and add the sugar, salt, pepper, and ginger. Pour in the vinegar and stir well to combine. Let the mustard stand 2 hours (or more) and stir again. If it is too thick, add water or additional vinegar, white wine, or dry sherry. The mustard can be eaten at this point; however, it will be *very* sharp. The mustard mellows nicely over time and is at its best at least a week or two after it is made.

Put the mustard in a sterile quart jar. Cover the jar with a lid and allow the mustard to mellow unrefrigerated. Add more liquid as needed. When you are ready to serve the mustard, taste and adjust the seasonings to your liking.

Note Any unused mustard can be stored indefinitely. It will continue to mellow as it ages.

above: The dreaded "children's table" has long been a part of the Thanksgiving holiday. It is easy to spot the child who thinks she should be with the adults.

Cranberry Orange Relish

Before the nineteenth century, cranberries were gathered where they grew wild in parts of New England, New Jersey, Oregon, Washington, and Wisconsin. They were first cultivated commercially in 1816 on Cape Cod, and a veritable boom occurred over the next several decades, as acre after acre of formerly unusable land was converted to profitable cranberry bogs. In 1912, the first commercially canned cranberry sauce was made in Hanson, Massachusetts. In 1930, a number of small canneries and processing plants combined to form Ocean Spray. Today, Americans consume more than 400 million pounds of cranberries a year, with 80 million pounds eaten during Thanksgiving week.

Versions of this recipe have been featured on bags of Ocean Spray cranberries for more than seventy years, and millions of schoolchildren across the country have made this no-cook cranberry relish for their family's Thanksgiving table.

MAKES ABOUT 4 CUPS

4 cups fresh cranberries
2 oranges, quartered, seeds removed
2 cups sugar

Place the cranberries and orange quarters in the bowl of a food processor and process with a metal blade until coarsely ground. (The original recipes used a food grinder.) Stir in sugar and chill. This relish will keep several weeks in a refrigerator.

Variations

Texas Cranberry Relish Add 1 or 2 serrano or jalapeño chilies, carefully seeded. *Gingered Cranberry Relish* Add 2 tablespoons crystallized ginger, minced finely. *Cranberry Orange Ambrosia* Add 1 cup shredded coconut. *Minted Cranberry Relish* Add 2 teaspoons fresh minced mint.

opposite: Generations of Americans have made this recipe for Cranberry Orange Relish. Today the old-fashioned grinder pictured has largely been replaced with the food processor. *Cranberry Orange Relish Recipe, 1954–1958.*

No Cooking!
CRANBERRY ORANGE RELISH

Put through food chopper:

1 lb. Ocean Spray fresh cranberries (4 cups).

2 oranges (including rind and pulp).

Stir in 2 cups sugar.

Store in refrigerator several hours so flavors will blend.

Makes 2 pints.

Keeps for weeks, if refrigerated.

How to serve:

Delicious with any meat; chicken, turkey, ham, or cold cuts.

Serve with cottage cheese for a delicious salad.

Fold one cup relish into raspberry gelatin just as it begins to jell. Makes delicious molded salad.

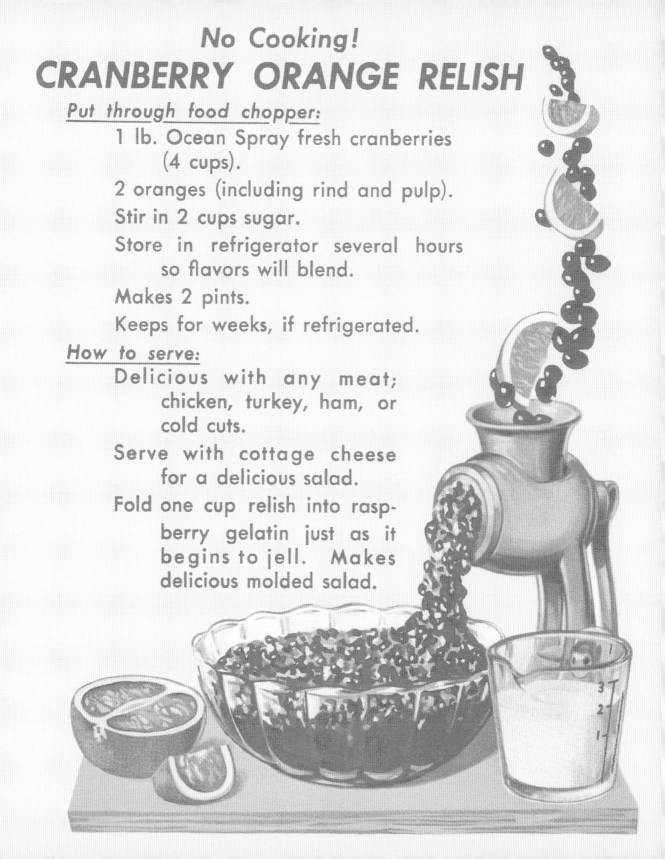

Cranberry Sauce

This recipe is adapted from Maria Parloa's *Appledore Cookbook* (1880). In Sandy Oliver's copy of the book, a previous owner inserted the word *brown* before the word *sugar,* which is a great idea. The amount of sugar in this recipe is reduced by half, making it a nice change from the sweeter commercial sauces. You may prefer to use a full 2 cups white sugar.

MAKES 2 CUPS

1 pound cranberries (about 4 cups)
1 cup water
1 cup firmly packed light brown sugar

Check the cranberries and remove any soft or brown ones. Put the good berries in a stainless-steel or enamel pan with the water. Sprinkle the brown sugar over them. Simmer gently, stirring frequently but gently, for about 30 minutes, or until the berries are soft and the sauce has a glossy appearance. Cool slightly and serve in a pretty glass bowl.

1880 Recipe

MARIA PARLOA, *THE APPLEDORE COOKBOOK*

Cranberry Sauce. Pick and wash the cranberries and put in the preserving kettle with half a pint of water to one quart of berries; now put the sugar on top of the berries, allowing a pint of sugar to a quart of berries. Set on the fire and stew about half an hour. Stir often to prevent burning. They will not need straining, and will preserve their rich color cooked this way. Never cook cranberries before putting in the sugar. Less sugar may be used if you do not want them very rich.

Cranberry Chutney

Chutney, a spicy vegetable relish, varies greatly from region to region in its native India. During their colonization of India, the English adopted and adapted the condiment. English versions tend to be a sweeter, more jam-like concoction featuring fruit. These anglicized adaptations became popular back home in England as well as in the United States during the late 1800s. Chutney was and is especially popular in the American South.

Chutneys made with cranberries are a late-twentieth-century addition to the Thanksgiving table. This chutney is wonderful alongside turkey and is especially good on the day-after turkey and stuffing sandwich.

MAKES 4 CUPS

    1 12-ounce bag cranberries, picked over and rinsed
    2 firm pears or Granny Smith apples, peeled, cored, and diced
  1/2 cup coarsely chopped dried apricots
    1 cup chopped onion (about 1 medium)
  1/2 cup firmly packed dark brown sugar
  1/3 cup cider vinegar
    2 tablespoons finely chopped crystallized ginger
  1/2 teaspoon red pepper flakes
  1/2 teaspoon whole mustard seeds
  1/2 teaspoon salt
  1/4 teaspoon ground coriander

Combine all of the ingredients in a heavy-bottomed saucepan. Bring to a boil, reduce heat to low, and simmer, stirring occasionally, for 25 minutes. Cool to room temperature or chill. This chutney keeps very well for several weeks in a sealed container in the refrigerator.

Desserts

Hard Sauce

Although hard sauce sometimes contains rum or brandy—that is, a hard liquor— its name derives from its hard consistency. It cannot be poured; it is more like a stiff frosting than a sauce, but when a dollop lands on a warm slice of plum pudding, it begins to soften and melt, adding a creamy sweetness to the spiciness of the pudding.

MAKES 1 CUP

4 tablespoons butter (½ stick), softened to room temperature
1 cup sifted confectioners' sugar
1 teaspoon rum, brandy, whiskey, or vanilla extract

Put the butter into a bowl and beat the confectioners' sugar into it gradually, using a wooden spoon or a handheld electric beater. When the butter mixture is well blended, add the liquor or the vanilla and beat until it is incorporated and the sauce is very smooth. Store in the refrigerator.

left: Re-created scene of a colonist at the window preparing a dish with eggs.

Plum Pudding

Despite its associations with Christmas, plum pudding appeared on nineteenth-century Thanksgiving tables. A rich plum pudding on a cold November day in the 1800s would have been a wonderful source of quick-to-burn calories to keep one warm on the sleigh trip back home.

Based on a recipe from Sarah Josepha Hale's *The Good Housekeeper* (1841), this plum pudding is dark, rich, and spicy, and it reflects a Temperance point of view, since it does not have a drop of brandy or rum in it. Other plum puddings of the era did, or were generously sprinkled with liquor, which helped tremendously in storing them. Many puddings proceeded directly to the table from the boiling pot. Others were stored for mellowing and then rewarmed, perhaps bathed in blue flames from warmed brandy poured over it and set afire for a memorable presentation. The adapted recipe below calls for a reduced amount of suet to meet modern tastes, though if you use the entire half pound recommended in the original, you will make a moister pudding. Suet, the rich crumbly fat from beef, is best purchased from a butcher. Supermarket suet is primarily sold as bird food and might not be fresh.

SERVES 12 TO 16

¼ pound suet
½ pound (1⅓ cups) raisins
½ pound (1⅔ cups) dried currants
1¾ cups bread crumbs
1 cup minus 2 tablespoons all-purpose flour
4 large eggs, beaten
1 teaspoon ground cinnamon
1 teaspoon ground nutmeg
1 teaspoon ground mace
1 teaspoon salt
½ cup sugar
2 tablespoons chopped mixed candied fruit peel
2 tablespoons chopped candied citron
½ cup milk
Hard Sauce (page 151) or sweetened whipped cream

Grease a 2-quart pudding mold (steamed pudding molds are available in specialty kitchen stores and catalogs) or a deep ceramic mixing bowl (often called a *pudding basin*). A steep heatproof metal or glass mixing bowl will do as well. If you are using a metal bowl, be sure to grease it very well.

Put a pot of water on to boil. Prepare a second pot that will hold your pudding mold or bowl as it steams. This pot must be large enough to hold the pudding mold or bowl with room around the sides for water. You also must be able to place a lid on the pot once the pudding is in it.

Grate the suet, removing any tough, stringy filaments, and place it in a large bowl. Add the raisins, currants, bread crumbs, flour, eggs, cinnamon, nutmeg, mace, salt, sugar, candied peel, and citron and stir together well. Gradually add the milk until the dough is evenly moist.

Place the mixture in the pudding bowl or mold. Cover the bowl (or mold, if it has no lid) with a piece of damp muslin and tie it in place. Place the pudding in the steaming pot and add boiling water to the pot halfway up the side of the bowl or mold. Cover the pot and steam for $1\frac{1}{2}$ to 2 hours, or until a knife inserted comes out clean and the surface of the pudding looks mostly dry. Keep hot water ready to add to the boiling pot in case the water evaporates. To serve, unmold the warm pudding onto a serving dish or platter. If you would like to flame the pudding, heat $\frac{1}{2}$ cup brandy or rum just to lukewarm. Drizzle the liquor over the pudding and ignite the fumes using a long-handled match. Be sure to stand back from the pudding when you ignite it. Serve the pudding sliced with hard sauce or whipped cream.

Indiana Persimmon Pudding

Persimmons ripen in the late fall. In the Midwest and the South, persimmon pudding is a favorite regional addition to many Thanksgiving tables. Like many dishes associated with Thanksgiving, persimmon pudding is a homey, old-fashioned comfort food.

This recipe is adapted from Jerry Lehman's favorite persimmon pudding. Jerry and his wife, Barb, grow their own native persimmons in Indiana; Barb has been making this recipe for about thirty years. Jerry says that aside from his favorite holiday dessert, persimmon pudding, his Thanksgiving is pretty typical. His wife also makes a couple of other unusual family desserts: grape pie and ground-cherry pie. Jerry says, "There are only three kinds of pie I eat: hot, cold, and old! My mother was a pie baker, and I was fortunate and married what I call Indiana's best pie baker. Have told her many times she should go into the business of selling pies to restaurants. She could get top dollar."

SERVES 8

5–6 *very* ripe persimmons
 ½ cup (1 stick) salted butter or margarine, melted
 ¼ cup blackberry wine or other sweet dessert wine
 ¾ cup buttermilk or milk
 1 large egg, beaten
 1 cup sugar
 1 cup all-purpose flour
 1 teaspoon baking powder
 ½ teaspoon baking soda
 ½ teaspoon ground cinnamon
 ¼ teaspoon salt
   Sweetened whipped cream or vanilla ice cream (optional)

Preheat the oven to 325°F. Grease and flour an 8 × 8-inch pan.

Cut off the top of 1 persimmon, scoop out the pulp, and mash it. Repeat until you have 1 cup persimmon pulp. (Don't worry if you have a few lumps.)

Place the persimmon pulp in a large bowl and add the melted butter, wine, buttermilk, egg, and sugar. Mix well. Hold a sifter or sieve over the persimmon mixture and spoon in the flour, baking powder, baking soda, cinnamon, and salt. Sift the flour mixture into the fruit mixture and blend until smooth.

Scrape the mixture into the prepared pan. Bake for about 45 minutes or until the edges are lightly browned and the center is set. The dish will puff slightly as it cooks.

Cool the pudding (it will sink slightly while cooling), cut into squares, and serve warm with whipped cream or vanilla ice cream.

❧ PERSIMMONS ❧

Plums there are of three sorts. The red and white are like our hedge plums, but the other which they call putchamins grow as high as a palmetto: the fruit is like a medlar; it is first green, then yellow, and red when it is ripe: if it be not ripe, it will draw a man's mouth awry, with much torment, but when it is ripe, it is as delicious as an apricot.

—JOHN SMITH, *GENERAL HISTORY OF VIRGINIA*, 1624

John Smith's "putchamins" were the hardy variety of persimmon native to America. For several centuries, native persimmons have turned up in American cookery in pies, beer, and even fudge.

Now many Americans in warmer climes grow imported Asian persimmons. In the fall, the fruit from these popularly cultivated Asian varieties (usually called Japanese persimmons) can be purchased in many grocery stores. Today's cooks can use the fruit from either the American or Asian persimmon to make delicious pies, cakes, and fudge—and, of course, a wonderful Thanksgiving pudding.

Arroz con Dulce
Coconut Rice Pudding

Willie Lebron lives in Massachusetts, but his family is originally from Puerto Rico. His family Thanksgiving, as made by his mother, Illuminada Gonzales, features many favorite Puerto Rican foods as well as a traditional turkey. The rest of the meal includes pernil (pork shoulder, recipe page 102), rice with pigeon peas, plantains, potato salad, empanadillas (meat pies), and pasteles (a mixture of boiled mashed plantain and a local root vegetable stuffed with peppers and pork). Willie says he could eat these for breakfast, lunch, and dinner, and they are, for him, the best part of Thanksgiving.

Instead of pies for dessert on Thanksgiving, Willie's family enjoys this wonderful Arroz con Dulce, a rich and sweet spiced rice pudding made with coconut milk. Mrs. Gonzalez begins with two whole coconuts, blends the milk and meat together, and then strains it through a cloth, but she provided a version for us that substitutes canned coconut milk. Traditionally, this pudding is spread thinly on a platter, allowed to cool, and then sliced and eaten cold. The Gonzalez-Lebron family prefers eating it warm with sweetened whipped cream. It is delicious both ways.

SERVES 6 TO 8

1 cup medium-grain white rice
1 13½-ounce can of coconut milk
¾ cup sugar
1 teaspoon vanilla extract
½ teaspoon salt
½ teaspoon ground ginger
½ teaspoon ground cinnamon
⅛ teaspoon ground cloves
½ cup raisins
  Sweetened whipped cream (optional)

Pour the rice into a medium mixing bowl, cover with cold water (at least 1 inch above the level of the rice), and soak for 2 hours. Drain the rice and discard the water.

Place the rice in a medium saucepan with 2 cups water, the coconut milk, sugar, vanilla, salt, ginger, cinnamon, cloves, and raisins. Stir to mix and place over medium heat. Bring the mixture to a boil, reduce the heat to a simmer, and cook, stirring occasionally, for 25 minutes, or until the rice is tender and the mixture is thick and creamy. You may have to stir almost continuously toward the end to keep the mixture from sticking. Serve warm with sweetened whipped cream.

NOTE To serve in the traditional manner, spread the rice pudding on a plate to the depth of about ½ inch, cover it with plastic wrap, and refrigerate it. When the rice pudding is cold, you can slice it like brownies.

above: Women in the nineteenth century worked for days in advance to prepare pies for the holiday. *Preparing for Thanksgiving* from *Ballou's Pictorial*, November 24, 1855.

Alabama Sweet Potato Pudding

Rich, creamy, and spicy sweet potato pudding (or *pone* as it is often called) is a southern classic. This recipe, which uses grated sweet potatoes, has been in the Westbrook family of southern Alabama for three or four generations. The Westbrooks serve it as part of their holiday dessert course, but in other southern families these puddings appear right alongside the turkey as a sweet side dish. Catherine Westbrook says of the dish, "The pudding or pone was not a recipe included in our holiday when I was growing up, but Mother revived the dish from the past about thirty years ago." Catherine's mother, Mary Catherine Franklin Luker, recalls that *her* mother sometimes made the pudding with molasses instead of sugar (molasses was considerably cheaper than sugar at the time) and that sometimes she added coconut. The Westbrook family has collected a wonderful book full of their family's favorite recipes, which include pecan pie, egg custard pie, sweet potato pie, and "Chicken and Dressing."

SERVES 6 TO 8

¾ cup sugar
½ teaspoon ground cinnamon
½ teaspoon ground nutmeg, preferably freshly grated
½ teaspoon salt
2 large eggs
1 13-ounce can of evaporated milk
½ cup milk
½ cup (1 stick) salted butter, melted
2 cups peeled, grated raw sweet potato (about 14 ounces whole sweet potato)

Preheat the oven to 350°F. Butter or spray a 1½-quart baking dish.

In a medium mixing bowl, combine the sugar, cinnamon, nutmeg, and salt. Beat in the eggs, mixing well. Stir in the evaporated milk, the fresh milk, and the butter. Mix in the sweet potato and pour into the prepared baking dish. Bake for 1 hour, or until the pudding is set.

right: This 1915 postcard shows stereotypical Pilgrims in buckled hats and black clothes. The reverse side features a handwritten Thanksgiving greeting—in Polish.

Thanksgiving Greetings

Pumpkin Cheesecake

Before the twentieth century, cheesecakes were made with curd cheese (such as ricotta or cottage cheese), eggs, sugar, spices, and often dried fruit. Modern European cheesecakes, like those made in Italy, are still based on this model. The classic New York–style cheesecake made with cream cheese is from the early twentieth century, appearing initially at Jewish delicatessens in Manhattan. According to Molly O'Neill in *The New York Cook Book*, "New York can't claim to be the birthplace of cheesecake. But historic detail has never stopped New Yorkers.... New Yorkers wave a dismissive hand ... and say that cheesecake wasn't really cheesecake until it was cheesecake in New York."

Pumpkin cheesecake is a late-twentieth-century Thanksgiving-themed variation on the popular dessert, and this version is especially good. The texture is fluffy and light, not as dense as most cheesecakes. The recipe is slightly adapted from a recipe called "Pumpkin Cheesecake with Bourbon Sour Cream Topping," which appeared in *Gourmet* (November 1990).

SERVES 12

For the crust

1 cup graham cracker crumbs
½ cup finely chopped pecans or walnuts
¼ cup firmly packed light brown sugar
¼ cup granulated sugar
¼ cup (½ stick) unsalted butter, melted and cooled

For the filling

1½ cups solid pack pumpkin
3 large eggs
1½ teaspoons ground cinnamon
1 teaspoon ground ginger
½ teaspoon freshly grated nutmeg
½ teaspoon salt
½ cup firmly packed light brown sugar

3 8-ounce packages of cream cheese, softened
½ cup granulated sugar
2 tablespoons heavy cream
1 tablespoon cornstarch
2 teaspoons vanilla extract
1 tablespoon bourbon liqueur or bourbon

For the topping

1¾ cups (1 16-ounce container) sour cream
3 tablespoons granulated sugar
1 tablespoon bourbon liqueur or bourbon, or to taste
16 pecan or walnut halves, for garnish

Butter a 9-inch springform pan and tightly wrap the bottom and sides with aluminum foil. In a medium bowl, thoroughly combine the cracker crumbs, pecans, brown sugar, and granulated sugar; stir in the butter. Press the mixture into the bottom and ½ inch up the side of the prepared pan. Chill the crust for 1 hour in the refrigerator (or 15 minutes in the freezer).

Place a rack in the center of the oven. Preheat the oven to 350°F.

In a medium bowl, whisk together the pumpkin, eggs, cinnamon, ginger, nutmeg, salt, and brown sugar. In a large bowl and using an electric mixer, cream together the cream cheese and granulated sugar. Beat in the cream, cornstarch, vanilla, bourbon liqueur, and the pumpkin mixture, and continue beating until smooth. Place the springform pan on a cookie sheet. Carefully pour the filling into the crust and bake the cheesecake for 50 to 55 minutes, or until the center is *just* set. Remove the pan to a rack to cool for 5 minutes. Do not turn off the oven. In a small bowl, whisk together the sour cream, sugar, and bourbon liqueur. Spread the sour cream mixture over the top of the cheesecake and bake for 5 minutes more. Transfer the pan to a rack to cool. Cover the cheesecake with foil and chill overnight. Gently run a sharp knife around the inside of the pan to loosen the crust. Carefully loosen and remove the side of the pan. Decorate the top of the cheesecake with the pecan halves.

Indian Pudding

Indian pudding, an American original, was common dessert fare well into the twentieth century. It has largely fallen out of favor in recent decades, replaced by showier, more vertical desserts that don't need to bake for several hours. Today it is considered a regional New England dish, but in earlier centuries, puddings like this one were made across the country and found in most American cookbooks. The first published recipe for Indian pudding appeared in 1796 in Amelia Simmons's *American Cookery,* but there is anecdotal evidence that the dish, made from the colonial staples of corn and molasses, was popular long before then.

Indian pudding has a spicy old-fashioned flavor and a homely, homey appearance. The pudding will often "break," making a watery whey that can just be stirred back into the pudding before serving.

Leftover pudding makes a great day-after-Thanksgiving breakfast food. Just warm it and serve with a generous splash of cream.

SERVES 6

- 1 cup cold water
- ½ cup yellow cornmeal
- 4 cups milk
- 1 large egg
- 3 tablespoons sugar
- ½ cup molasses
- 2 tablespoons (¼ stick) salted butter
- 1 teaspoon ground cinnamon
- 1 teaspoon ground ginger
- ½ teaspoon freshly grated or ground nutmeg
- ¼ teaspoon salt
    Vanilla ice cream (optional)

Preheat the oven to 300°F. Grease a 1½-quart ovenproof dish or crock.

Place the water in a small bowl and gradually whisk in the cornmeal until the mixture is completely smooth.

Scald 3 cups of the milk in a heavy saucepan and stir the cornmeal mixture into the boiling milk. Boil gently, stirring frequently, for 15 minutes, until the mixture is thickened.

Remove from the heat. Beat the egg in a small bowl. Stir some of the hot cornmeal mixture into the beaten egg, a spoonful at a time, until you have added about ½ cup. Return the egg mixture to the saucepan and stir in the sugar, molasses, butter, cinnamon, ginger, nutmeg, and salt. Pour the mixture into the prepared dish. Bake for 30 minutes.

Remove from the oven and gently pour the remaining 1 cup of cold milk over the top of the pudding. Do not stir in. Bake for 2 hours longer, or until set. Serve warm with a splash of cream or vanilla ice cream.

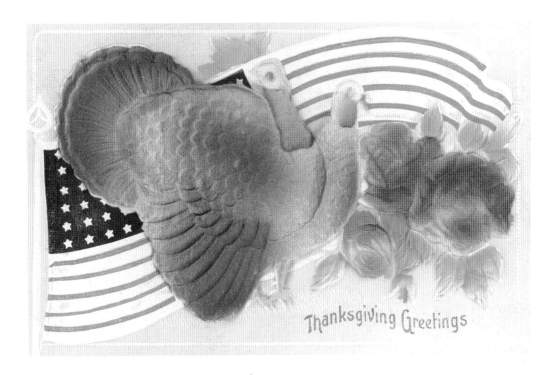

above: In this wonderfully gaudy WWI-era postcard, Thanksgiving is infused with patriotism.

Four-Milk Flan

Flans (including pumpkin flans) are part of the Thanksgiving dessert menu for many people of Hispanic descent. The flan featured below is part of the holiday menu for Soledad Lopez, the owner of Guelaguetza Restaurant in West Los Angeles, California. Special thanks to food writer Amelia Saltsman, our correspondent in California, for Soledad's story and recipe.

Soledad comes from Matatlan, Oaxaca, in Mexico. She arrived in the United States in 1982 and about three years later, she and her family started celebrating Thanksgiving. "My sister and I saw everyone having Thanksgiving. Everyone had the day off. It was like Christmas to us. So we started having tamales. We added turkey a few years later.... Oaxacans don't know how to make turkey in the oven. We make it on the stove, as a *caldo* [boiled to yield soup and meat] with mole, and serve it with white rice." Mole is an incredibly flavorful Mexican sauce used on many meat dishes.

"We think of Thanksgiving like celebrating another *Navidad* [Christmas] or *Día de los Muertos* [Day of the Dead]. We start with a small drink of mezcal in the living room, then go to the table where we drink hot chocolate with *pan de yema* [an egg bread, like brioche, that is dipped in the hot chocolate]. We spend maybe forty minutes talking and enjoying the chocolate. Then we clear away all these things and set out the turkey mole with tortillas and rice.... For dessert, we have little pastries called *dulces regionales,* a special *flan Napolitano* made with four kinds of milk, and Jell-O from Oaxaca." Soledad's recipe makes a delicate flan with lots of caramel syrup. Depending on how sweet you want your flan, use between three-quarters and one entire can of the sweetened condensed milk. Soledad uses the lesser amount.

SERVES 12

1½ cups sugar
1 14-ounce can sweetened condensed milk
2 12-ounce cans evaporated milk
1 cup regular milk
½ cup half-and-half
4 large eggs
1 teaspoon ground cinnamon
1 teaspoon vanilla extract

Preheat the oven to 350°F. Heat a large light-colored skillet over medium heat. When the pan is hot, reduce the heat to low and add the sugar. Cook, stirring occasionally, until the sugar is melted and amber-colored, about 10 minutes. Immediately and carefully pour this syrup into a shallow 2-quart baking dish and set aside to cool.

Place the remaining ingredients in the bowl of a mixer. Beat on medium speed for 5 minutes. Pour this mixture over the cooled syrup. Place the baking dish in a larger pan, set it in the center of the oven, and pour water into the larger pan to come about halfway up the sides of the baking dish holding the flan. Bake until the top is golden brown and the custard is somewhat set, 45 to 60 minutes. (The flan will jiggle when first out of the oven but get firmer after refrigeration.) Remove from the oven and cool completely. Refrigerate the flan until firm or overnight. Unmold onto a serving platter and scrape any remaining syrup from the pan onto the flan. Slice to serve.

above: Martha Stewart had nothing on this family, who decorated their holiday table and chandelier with garlands of cranberries. *George Leitch Carving the Turkey*, 1905, from the McFadden family album.

Libby's Famous Pumpkin Pie

For many Americans, Thanksgiving is as much about pumpkins as it is about turkey. Without question, pumpkin pie is *the* classic Thanksgiving dessert, and for generations, Libby's Famous Pumpkin Pie has been the favorite of millions of Americans. In fact, it is hard to think of another recipe that is as popular. The folks at Libby's estimate that more than 50 million pies are made from their pumpkin products every year. The first can of Libby's pumpkin was processed and sold in 1929. The classic recipe first appeared on the label in 1950 and has remained virtually unchanged since. It is reprinted here courtesy of Nestlé USA, Inc.

SERVES 8

- ¾ cup sugar
- ½ teaspoon salt
- 1 teaspoon ground cinnamon
- ½ teaspoon ground ginger
- ¼ teaspoon ground cloves
- 2 large eggs
- 1 can (15 ounces) Libby's 100% Pure Pumpkin
- 1 12-ounce can evaporated milk
- 1 unbaked 9-inch piecrust (page 167), made in a deep-dish plate, or a purchased deep-dish (4-cup volume) unbaked piecrust
  Sweetened whipped cream (optional)

Preheat the oven to 425°F.

Mix the sugar, salt, cinnamon, ginger, and cloves in a small bowl. Beat the eggs in a large bowl. Stir in the pumpkin and the sugar-spice mixture. Gradually stir in the evaporated milk. Pour the filling into the piecrust. Bake the pie for 15 minutes. Reduce the oven temperature to 350°F and bake for an additional 40 to 50 minutes or until a knife inserted near the center comes out clean. Cool the pie on a wire rack for 2 hours. Serve immediately or refrigerate. To serve, slice and top with whipped cream.

All-Purpose Piecrust

This is a good basic pastry that will work for all of the pies in this book. If you are making your first attempt at piecrust, however, you may want to look at one of the many pie cookbooks in print for a detailed description of the process. If making pastry is not in your Thanksgiving plans, you can purchase acceptable ready-made piecrusts at your local market.

MAKES 1 9-INCH SINGLE-CRUST PIE;
DOUBLE THE AMOUNTS FOR A 9-INCH DOUBLE-CRUST PIE

1½ cups all-purpose flour
½ teaspoon salt
½ cup cold unsalted butter (1 stick) or shortening, or a mix of the two
3–5 tablespoons ice water

THE GREAT PUMPKIN COOKBOOK

A Harvest of LIBBY'S Favorite Recipes

Using a fork, mix the flour and salt together in a medium bowl. With a pastry blender or two knives, cut the butter or shortening into the dry ingredients until the mixture resembles coarse bread crumbs. Drizzle the ice water over the mixture, 1 tablespoon at a time, and toss the mixture with a fork until the pastry begins to come together in moist clumps. (You want the dough just moist enough to hold together when pressed.) Gather the pastry into a ball, flatten it into a disk, wrap it securely in plastic wrap, and place it in the refrigerator. Chill the dough for at least 30 minutes before rolling out. (The dough can be kept refrigerated for 2 days before using. Well-wrapped disks can be frozen for several months.)

left: No pumpkin pie recipe is as popular as the one on the back of each and every can of Libby's pumpkin. That recipe and many others are featured in Libby's cookbook, *The Great Pumpkin Cookbook*.

Old-Fashioned Pumpkin Pie

Based on a recipe in Lettice Bryan's *Kentucky Housewife* (1839), this is a classic stewed pumpkin pie, with a lovely spiciness from cloves and an enticing aroma from brandy. There were, in early America, versions of pumpkin pie made with sliced raw pumpkin, just as we make apple pies today.

Pumpkins, as prolific as their cousin zucchini, proved useful to the English and other settlers in America. They were dried or stored whole in cool, dry places in the house until wanted. They were used as a side dish for meat, and by the nineteenth century, pumpkin was one of the most common pie fillings. The secret to making a good pumpkin pie from fresh pumpkin is to drain the pulp well after cooking. Mash it, then let it sit in a sieve for 10 minutes to allow most of the water to drip away before mixing it with the rest of the ingredients.

SERVES 8

1 cup milk or half-and-half
1 tablespoon butter
½ cup light brown sugar, packed
2 cups homemade stewed pumpkin (or 1 15-ounce can plain pumpkin purée)
2 eggs, beaten
¼ cup brandy
1 teaspoon ground cinnamon
1 teaspoon ground or freshly grated nutmeg
¼–½ teaspoon ground cloves (clove lovers will want to use the larger amount)
¼ teaspoon salt
1 unbaked 9-inch piecrust (page 167)

Preheat the oven to 350°F.

Put the milk in a saucepan with the butter and the sugar and warm them together until the butter melts. Add the warmed milk to the pumpkin in a large bowl. Add the beaten eggs, brandy, cinnamon, nutmeg, cloves, and salt and mix until it becomes a smooth batter. Line a 9-inch pie plate with the crust, crimping the edges, and then pour in the pumpkin mixture. Bake for 1 hour or until a knife inserted in the center comes out clean.

Massachusetts Marlboro Pudding (Pie)

This recipe for a stewed apple pie is adapted from one by Amelia Simmons, who authored the first American cookbook, *American Cookery*, in 1796. The pie was popular in Amelia's day and remained so in Massachusetts well into the twentieth century. In her book *How America Eats* (1960), Clementine Paddleford says that it was a popular Thanksgiving dessert around Boston, where "four kinds of pie were traditional ... mince, cranberry, pumpkin, and a kind called Marlborough, a glorification of everyday apple."

Marlboro Pie has enjoyed a recent revival. After television weatherman Al Roker featured Old Sturbridge Village's version of this pie on a Thanksgiving show, it has been one of the Massachusetts museum's most requested recipes. The combination of stewed apples, lemon, sherry, and cream makes for a deliciously different apple pie. Lemon does not appear in Miss Simmons's original recipe, but it is in other Marlboro Pie recipes and is a nice complement to the other flavors.

SERVES 8

　1　lemon
　1　cup plain unsweetened applesauce
½　cup sugar
½　cup sweet or cream sherry
　6　tablespoons (¾ stick) salted butter, melted
　4　large eggs, well beaten
½　cup heavy cream
½　teaspoon grated nutmeg, or to taste
　1　unbaked 9-inch piecrust (page 167)
　　Sweetened whipped cream (optional)

Preheat the oven to 350°F.

Grate the zest (the yellow part of the rind) from the lemon into a large mixing bowl. Squeeze the juice from the lemon into the bowl. Add the applesauce, sugar, sherry, butter, eggs, cream, and nutmeg and mix well. Pour into the unbaked piecrust and bake about 1 hour or until set. Cool and serve with sweetened whipped cream.

Sliced Apple Pie

The quality of an apple pie depends heavily on the apples you use. McIntoshes make a soft filling; Granny Smiths, a firm, almost dry filling. You can use a mixture of them if you like, or use Cortlands, Romes, or whatever your favorites are. Add more sugar to the recipe if you like sweet pie; or consider using light brown or raw sugar.

This is an updated version of an 1883 recipe contributed by Mrs. D. Burton to *Practical Housekeeping* by the Buckeye Publishing Company. A good many apple pie recipes from the 1800s call for stewed apples, which perhaps explains why this recipe is entitled "Sliced Apple Pie." (For a stewed apple pie, see page 169.)

SERVES 8

Pastry for 1 9-inch double-crust pie (page 167)
¼ cup sugar
3 teaspoons ground cinnamon
3 tablespoons all-purpose flour
About 2 pounds apples (7–10), cored and sliced (paring optional)
Ground or freshly grated nutmeg (optional)
4 tablespoons butter, cut into pieces
2 teaspoons cream (any type), for glazing the top of the pie (optional)

Preheat the oven to 375°F.

Line a 9-inch pie plate with one of the piecrusts. Mix the sugar, cinnamon, and flour together in a small bowl. Slice one third of the apples directly into the piecrust, sprinkle on a little water, add one third of the sugar mixture, grate on a little nutmeg, and add a few pieces of the butter. Repeat twice more, until the pie plate is full. Top with the remaining piecrust and crimp the edges. Slash the top; glaze, if you wish, with a little cream. Bake for 10 minutes, then reduce the heat to 350°F and bake for 35 to 40 minutes, or until you can see juices bubbling through the hole in the top.

Southern Sweet Potato Pie

Sweet potato pies have been made in the South for centuries. According to John Edgerton in *Southern Food: At Home, On the Road, In History,* the prototype for the modern custardy sweet potato pie likely came from an early-twentieth-century Tuskegee Institute Bulletin by George Washington Carver, who was a big promoter of the sweet potato. Today, sweet potato pies are a staple of southern cookbooks and a favorite dessert at Thanksgiving time. This recipe is from Marcia Hix, an extraordinary cook and caterer who spent a number of years living and cooking in the South. Although she now lives in Massachusetts, she learned to cook many of her most requested recipes, including southern barbecue, raised (angel) biscuits, and this sweet potato pie, while she was living in the Carolinas. On Thanksgiving, in addition to other desserts, Marcia makes her two favorite pies, Shoo-Fly Pie and this Sweet Potato Pie.

SERVES 8

- 4 tablespoons (½ stick) salted butter, at room temperature
- ¾ cup packed light brown sugar
- 2 tablespoons honey
- 1½ teaspoons lemon juice
- 1½ teaspoons orange juice
- 1½ cups cooked, mashed sweet potatoes (about 2 large)
- 2 large eggs, slightly beaten
- ½ cup canned evaporated milk
- 1½ teaspoons grated lemon zest
- 1½ teaspoons grated orange zest
- 1 teaspoon vanilla extract
- ½ teaspoon salt
- ½ teaspoon freshly grated or ground nutmeg
- ½ teaspoon ground cinnamon
- ¼ teaspoon ground allspice
- 1 unbaked 9-inch piecrust (see page 167)
  Sweetened whipped cream (optional)

Preheat the oven to 450°F.

In a large mixing bowl, using a mixer, cream the butter and brown sugar. Beat in the honey and the lemon and orange juices. Add the sweet potatoes and eggs and beat. Add the evaporated milk, lemon and orange zest, vanilla, salt, nutmeg, cinnamon, and allspice and beat until smooth.

Pour the mixture into the piecrust. Bake for 15 minutes, reduce the heat to 325°F, and continue to bake for 30 minutes more, or until a knife inserted in the middle comes out clean. Serve with whipped cream, if desired

❧ SWEET POTATOES AND YAMS ❧

Sweet potatoes are the large tuberous roots of a vine native to Peru. By the time Europeans arrived in the late fifteenth century, sweet potatoes were being cultivated by the Native People in the Caribbean and in what is now Louisiana. Despite the name, sweet potatoes are not botanically related to white potatoes at all. Of the many varieties of sweet potato available today, the two most common in American markets are very different from one another. One has a thin yellow skin with cream-colored flesh. When cooked, this variety is dry and firm, like a baked white potato. The other is much darker in color and when cooked has a moist, soft, orange-colored flesh. This variety is often marketed as a "yam."

The true yam is a large tuber native to Asia and Africa, and most Americans have never tasted one. Yams are starchier and less sweet than sweet potatoes. When African slaves were brought to the South, the Guinea word for "something to eat," *nyani,* was attached to the sweet potato and they began to be called yams. The name caught on, particularly in the Deep South, where sweet potatoes were and are a dietary staple. To confuse matters a bit more, modern Louisiana sweet potato producers have officially adopted the name *yam* for their moist orange-fleshed sweet potatoes to differentiate them from the paler-fleshed variety.

Apple Almond Crostata

This delightfully Italian Thanksgiving dessert comes from Laura Carroll of Largo, Florida. It was originally from her mother's aunt Elvira "Vera" Zanotti, whose family came from Brescia in the Lombardy region of Italy. Elvira immigrated to Pittsburgh and made this recipe frequently, varying it with fruits in season. The recipe was passed on in the family and quickly became a favorite. The delectable and tender biscotti cookie crust and apple and almond topping will make it a memorable addition to your Thanksgiving table.

While the dessert was made for many occasions, Laura was the first to incorporate it into the Thanksgiving meal. "I always make the desserts, and I usually make this crostata, along with pumpkin pie and sweet potato pie. My family's Thanksgiving has always included the traditional turkey and stuffing, homemade cranberry sauce, and fresh green beans and salad, plus spinach with goat cheese, since that's my favorite vegetable. Since I became a vegetarian two years ago I eat all of the vegetable-based dishes and make stuffing made with vegetable broth."

SERVES 8

⅓ cup slivered almonds
2 cups all-purpose flour
1 cup sugar
2 teaspoons baking powder
¼ teaspoon salt
½ cup (1 stick) cold butter
2 eggs, lightly beaten
1 teaspoon almond or vanilla extract
1 10-ounce jar fruit-sweetened apricot jam
2 large apples, peeled and thinly sliced (about 2 cups)
  Vanilla ice cream or sweetened whipped cream

Preheat the oven to 325°F. Place the almond slivers on a small baking sheet and toast them for 10 minutes. Set aside.

Combine the flour, sugar, baking powder, and salt in a medium bowl. Cut the butter into small pieces and add it to the flour mixture, crumbling it with your fingers until the mixture resembles coarse cornmeal. In small bowl, mix the beaten eggs and the almond extract together. Add to the flour mixture and stir to blend. Flour your hands well (the dough will be very moist) and form the dough into a ball. Pat about two thirds of the dough into a 10-inch tart pan or springform pan.

Melt the jam in a small pan. Arrange the apple slices on the dough. Pour the melted jam over the fruit. (If you prefer, you can mix the jam with the apples before placing them in the pie pan.) Sprinkle the toasted almond slivers over the apples. Flour your hands and roll the remaining dough into long strips (about a pencil's thickness) on a well-floured surface. Place the strips over the filling in a latticework pattern. Press the ends of each strip into the dough at the edge of the pie pan. These strips will spread during baking. Bake 45 to 50 minutes, until the crust is golden and lightly browned. Serve warm or cold with vanilla ice cream or whipped cream.

above: An autumn scene in the 1627 Pilgrim Village at Plimoth Plantation

Old-Fashioned Mincemeat Pie

The following recipe, based on one in Marian Harland's *Dinner Year-Book* (1878), makes spectacular mincemeat, redolent of sherry and brandy, rich and dark, best served warm. What a pity we have relegated mincemeat pie to the end of the meal, when it would be so good alongside the turkey, where it was served in the eighteenth century.

This pie actually has meat in it, as did most mincemeat pies until fairly recently. About a hundred years ago, meatless versions began to appear in cookbooks, and now virtually all modern commercial ones contain no meat.

Mincemeat was a convenient and delicious way to preserve meat, suet, and apples. It was very nearly fast food, standing ready to be scooped out and baked up fresh in a crust—hence the comment at the end of the 1878 recipe noting that the mincemeat will keep all winter "if not used up." Instructions in historical cookbooks cautioning the cook to seed the raisins remind us that the little seedless raisins we have today are relatively recent, available for only a little over a hundred years. Before then the raisins were quite large, the size of a grape, dried, with the seeds still in them. Memoirs of people who grew up in the early nineteenth century often speak of helping with the seeding of raisins, which required pinching the raisin and picking out the seed, an ideal activity for small fingers.

SERVES 8

   Pastry for 1 double-crust 9-inch pie (page 167)
4 cups Mincemeat (recipe follows)
1 teaspoon milk or cream, for glaze (optional)

Preheat the oven to 450°F.

Roll out half of the pastry dough and line a 9-inch pie plate with it. Lay 4 cups of the mincemeat in the dough, and, for a classic pie, make a lattice top with the remaining dough. Or, if time is short, roll out another round of pastry for the top and crimp all around. Make a few slashes in the top and glaze with a little cream or milk if you wish. Bake the pie for 10 minutes, and then reduce the temperature to 350°F and bake for an additional 30 minutes.

Mincemeat

    1 pound lean beef (chuck is good)
    ¼ pound beef suet
  2½ pounds apples
    1 pound raisins
    ½ pound golden raisins
    1 pound dried currants
    ¾ cup finely chopped candied citron
    1 tablespoon cinnamon
    ½ whole nutmeg, freshly grated, or 1½ teaspoons ground nutmeg
    1 tablespoon ground mace
  1½ teaspoons ground cloves
  1½ teaspoons ground allspice
  1½ teaspoons salt
  1¼ pounds brown sugar
    1 cup cream sherry
    1 cup brandy

Boil the beef about 30 minutes in barely enough water to cover it. Remove it from the heat and, when cool enough to handle, pulse it in a food processor, chop it in a wooden bowl with a chopping knife, or put it through a food mill fitted with the coarsest blade. The result should be small but not powdery bits of meat. Put it into a large bowl. Grate the suet with a fairly fine grating blade in the food processor or on a box grater and mix it evenly into the meat.

Peel (if you wish) and core the apples, chop them as you did the meat, and add to the meat and suet. Then add the raisins, currants, citron, cinnamon, nutmeg, mace, cloves, allspice, salt, and brown sugar and mix, blending them evenly together. Gradually add the sherry and brandy and stir until the mixture looks moist. Let the mincemeat stand in a unheated room or refrigerator for at least 24 hours before using, stirring occasionally. The fruits will absorb the liquor. Stored in a covered crock in a cool place (or refrigerator), mincemeat will keep for a winter's worth of spectacular pies.

above: The makers of Karo corn syrup are largely responsible for the creation and popularity of pecan pie.

Classic Karo Pecan Pie

The roots of the pecan pie are a mystery. One of the most famous of American desserts, the pie recipe surprisingly does not exist in any recorded form until the late 1920s. By the 1940s, southerners had claimed it as their own (after all, pecans are grown in the South), and John Edgerton, in *Southern Food,* theorizes that the pie descended from nineteenth-century southern molasses pie recipes.

Whatever its origins, pecan pie did not become truly popular until it was combined with commercial corn syrup in the 1930s. According to the folks at Karo, which manufactures corn syrup, the wife of a Karo company sales executive was the first to make a pie from a mixture of corn syrup, sugar, eggs, vanilla, and pecans. In the 1940s, a corn syrup version of pecan pie appeared in virtually every mainstream American cookbook (and in absolutely every southern one, where it is often called Karo Pie). Choose dark corn syrup for a deeper flavor.

SERVES 8

    3 large eggs
    1 cup dark or light corn syrup
    1 cup sugar
    2 tablespoons (¼ stick) butter, melted
    1 teaspoon vanilla extract
 1½ cup pecans, chopped or whole
    1 unbaked 9-inch piecrust (page 167)
       Vanilla ice cream or sweetened whipped cream

Preheat the oven to 350°F.

In a medium bowl, beat the eggs and add the corn syrup, sugar, butter, and vanilla. Stir until well blended. Stir in the pecans. Pour the filling into the unbaked pie crust. Bake for 50 to 55 minutes. The pie is done when a knife inserted in the center of the pie comes out clean. Cool on a wire rack. Serve with vanilla ice cream or whipped cream.

Variation

For chocolate pecan pie, add two 1-ounce squares of unsweetened chocolate, melted, to the filling before you add the pecans. Proceed with the rest of the recipe as written.

Pear Mincemeat Pie

Mincemeat pies were originally just that—meat chopped with suet and seasoned with dried fruit, sugar, spices, and orange peels. These fancy main-dish pies were a part of the English Christmas tradition since the Middle Ages. While the name has stayed the same, the ingredients have changed over time. By the 1800s, brandy, wine, or other liquors were often included, and minced pie took a turn toward dessert. By the first half of the twentieth century, "mock" mincemeat, which contained no meat, began to outstrip the old-fashioned meat pies. Today, "real" mincemeat has all but vanished from mainstream cookbooks. And on Thanksgiving Day, the once-traditional mincemeat pie is served much less frequently than it was even fifty years ago.

All that being said, this is a lovely recent (1990) take on meatless mincemeat pie from *Thanksgiving Dinner* by Anthony Dias Blue and Kathryn Blue. It has a wonderful flavor, and if you don't want to go to the trouble of making a pie, it makes a great topping for vanilla ice cream—which is rarely said of mincemeat with meat! The filling can be made a week in advance and stored at room temperature. This gives the complex flavors a chance to develop.

SERVES 8

 1 lemon
½ cup firmly packed dark brown sugar
 1 cup coarsely chopped currants
½ cup coarsely chopped golden raisins
 1 cup coarsely chopped cranberries
 2 pounds firm pears, peeled, cored, and coarsely chopped
¾ cup apple cider
 2 tablespoons unsulfured molasses
 1 teaspoon vanilla extract
 1 teaspoon ground cinnamon
½ teaspoon freshly grated nutmeg
¼ teaspoon ground ginger
¼ teaspoon ground allspice
    Pinch of freshly ground black pepper
 1 cup walnuts

⅓ cup Calvados or apple brandy
2 tablespoons unsalted butter
   Pastry for 1 double-crust 9-inch pie (page 167)
1 egg white, lightly beaten

Slice the peel from the lemon with a sharp knife or a vegetable peeler. Cut off any of the white pith from the pieces of peel. Mince the peel. After cutting away the pith, chop the lemon coarsely. Put the minced peel and the lemon into a 2-quart saucepan with the brown sugar.

In the bowl of a food processor fitted with a metal blade, place the currants, raisins, cranberries, pears, cider, molasses, vanilla, cinnamon, nutmeg, ginger, allspice, and pepper. Pulse 4 or 5 times. Add to the saucepan containing the lemon.

Place the saucepan over medium heat and bring to a simmer. Reduce the heat and continue to simmer for 30 minutes, stirring occasionally.

Preheat the oven or a toaster oven to 350°F. Toast the walnuts for 20 minutes. Chop coarsely.

Add the brandy to the raisin-cranberry mixture and simmer for an additional 5 minutes. Remove from the heat and stir in the walnuts and butter. (At this point you can store the cooled filling for up to a week in a large covered container.)

Line a 9-inch pie plate with a circle of piecrust dough. Pierce the bottom several times with a fork. Fill—but don't overfill—with the mincemeat. Top with the other circle of dough, crimping the edges and piercing the top several times with a small, sharp knife. Brush the top surface with the egg white.

Bake until the crust is deep golden brown, about 40 minutes. Cool to room temperature before serving.

Texas Buttermilk Pie

The Southern Thanksgiving tradition includes a wide variety of old-fashioned pies such as chess, molasses, pecan, and buttermilk. Local and family recipes for each of these pies appear frequently in the many community cookbooks that are a vital part of the landscape of Southern food. While some of these pies are relative newcomers, buttermilk pie has been around for more than a century.

This recipe comes from Alice Arndt, a food historian, author of *Seasoning Savvy,* and editor of *Culinary Biographies.* Alice lives in Houston, Texas, where buttermilk pie is a state favorite. (There were two recipes for buttermilk pie in *The First Texas Cookbook* printed in 1883.) In her recipe, Alice says she "adds lemon juice and lemon peel even though it's not traditional. The stuff labeled *buttermilk* that we buy today in the supermarket lacks the nice tang of real buttermilk."

SERVES 8

½ cup (1 stick) unsalted butter, at room temperature
1¾ cups sugar
4 large eggs
2 tablespoons all-purpose flour
Pinch of salt
1 cup buttermilk
1 teaspoon lemon juice
½ teaspoon finely grated lemon zest
1 teaspoon vanilla extract
¼ teaspoon freshly grated nutmeg
Pastry for 1 double-crust 9-inch pie (page 167)

Preheat the oven to 325°F.

In a large bowl, cream the butter and sugar together. Beat in the eggs, one at a time. Add the flour and salt. In a medium bowl or a 2-cup measure, mix the buttermilk, lemon juice, lemon zest, vanilla, and nutmeg. Pour the buttermilk mixture into the mixing bowl and blend well.

Pour the mixture into the unbaked piecrust and bake until a sharp knife inserted just off center comes out clean. Cool and serve.

Cranberry Pear Pie

"As American as cranberry pie" makes much more sense than the usual saying. Cranberries, after all, are native to America, and pies or tarts made from them appear in colonial records as early as 1672. Before the middle of the nineteenth century, when they began to be shipped to cities and larger towns, cranberries, like most fresh produce, were a local item eaten in the places where they grew wild—in parts of New England, New Jersey, Oregon, Washington, and Wisconsin. Even today, fresh cranberries are still very much a seasonal fruit, and if you want to cook with them after the holidays you need to freeze them while they are around.

This recipe comes from Sue Mello, who has been making this pie for Thanksgiving for about twenty years. The rest of her meal combines a little of her Portuguese heritage with a traditional Thanksgiving dinner: "I roast a turkey and stuff it with a bread stuffing with a little bit of ground Portuguese chouriço sausage in it. I have always loved a good chestnut stuffing, but if I want some I have to make it in addition to the other. Everyone says they like the chestnut stuffing but they feel like something's missing without the chouriço stuffing! Also, it wouldn't be Thanksgiving at my house without lots of mashed potatoes, green beans, butternut squash, turnip and carrots, fresh rolls and butter, cranberry sauce, olives, pickles, and some gravy. We have that meal around one in the afternoon, and a couple of hours later we're usually ready for the desserts! Along with the cranberry pear pie I usually serve apple pie and/or cheesecake, and my kids insist on rice pudding from my mother-in-law's recipe. If I even try to vary from that menu I catch a lot of flak!" The ruby-red color of this pie is just beautiful when sliced, and the filling has a nice tartness that is the perfect foil for vanilla ice cream. It was a favorite of our pie tasters, who pronounced it "perfect."

SERVES 8

1½ cups sugar
¼ cup cornstarch
½ teaspoon ground cinnamon
3 cups fresh cranberries, rinsed and picked over
2 cups pared, sliced pears (2 large)
   Pastry for 1 double-crust 9-inch pie (page 167)
   Vanilla ice cream (optional)

In a medium bowl, mix together the sugar, cornstarch, and cinnamon. Set aside.

In a medium saucepan, combine the cranberries and 1 cup water; bring to a boil over high heat. Reduce the heat to low and simmer for 3 minutes. Add the sugar mixture to the saucepan and stir constantly, cooking until the mixture bubbles. Remove the pan from the heat, gently stir in the pears, and allow the mixture to cool to room temperature.

Preheat the oven to 400°F. Place a piece of foil on the bottom oven rack to catch any drips from the baking pie.

Line a 9-inch pie plate with a circle of piecrust dough. Pour or spoon the cooled cranberry mixture into the bottom of the piecrust. Lightly moisten the rim of the crust with cold water. For a spectacular presentation, you can make a latticework top crust (see Note). Otherwise, loosely drape the top crust over the cranberries, leaving a ½-inch overhang. Turn the edge of the top crust under the edge of the bottom and crimp with your fingers to seal. Cut several slashes in the top crust to release steam as the pie bakes. Bake for 35 to 40 minutes, or until the crust is golden brown and the juices are bubbling. Don't worry if some of the juices escape as the pie bakes.

Serve warm with vanilla ice cream, if desired.

NOTE To make a lattice top crust, cut rolled-out dough into ½-inch-wide strips. Arrange 5 to 6 dough strips across the top of the filling. Arrange an equal number of dough strips at a right angle to the first strips, weaving them if you wish. Trim the strips even with the dough overhang on the bottom crust. Tuck the ends of the strips and the overhang under; press to seal, and then flute the edges.

Bibliography

Due to space considerations we were not able to include all original period recipes alongside their modern "translations." They are available on Plimoth Plantation's website at www.plimoth.org/givingthanks.

A., W. *A Book of Cookrye*, 1591.

Anderson, Jean. *The American Century Cookbook*. New York: Clarkson N. Potter, 1997.

Appelbaum, Diana K. *Thanksgiving, An American Holiday, An American History*. New York: Facts on File, 1984.

Arndt, Alice. *Seasoning Savvy*. Binghamton, N.Y.: Haworth Press, 1999.

Baker, James W., and Elizabeth Brabb. *Thanksgiving Cookery*. New York: Brick Tower Press, 1994.

Batra, Neelam. *Chilis to Chutneys: American Home Cooking with the Flavors of India*. London: HarperCollins, 1998.

Beard, James. *American Cookery*. Boston: Little, Brown & Company, 1980.

Blue, Anthony Dias, and Kathryn Blue. *Thanksgiving Dinner*. New York: HarperCollins, 1990.

Bowles, Ella Shannon, and Dorothy Towle. *Secrets of New England Cooking*. New York: M. Barrows and Company, 1947.

Bradford, William. *Of Plymouth Plantation, 1620–1647*. Edited by Samuel E. Morison. New York: Alfred A. Knopf, 1952.

Brown, Cora. *America Cooks: Favorite Recipes from 48 States*. Garden City, N.Y.: Halcyon House, 1949, 1940.

Brown, Helen Evans. *Holiday Cookbook*. Boston: Little, Brown & Company, 1952.

———. *West Coast Cookbook*. Knopf, 1991.

Bryan, Lettice. *Kentucky Housewife*, 1839. Columbia, S.C.: University of South Carolina Press, 1991 (reprint).

Buckeye Cookery and Practical Housekeeping, rev. ed. Minneapolis: Buckeye Publishing Co., 1880.

Channing, Mary J. "Sixty Years Ago," *The Youth's Companion*. December 1894.

Cressy, David. *Bonfires and Bells: National Memory and the Protestant Calendar in Elizabethan and Stuart England*. Berkeley: University of California Press, 1989.

Davidson, Alan. *The Oxford Companion to Food*. Oxford: Oxford University Press, 1999.

Dawson, Thomas. *The Second Part of the Good Housewives Jewell*, 1597.

Dennis, Matthew. *Red, White and Blue Letter Days: An American Calendar*. Ithaca, N.Y.: Cornell University Press, 2002.

Digbie, Kenelme. *The Closet Opened*. London, 1669.

Edgerton, John. *Southern Food: At Home, On the Road, in History*. New York: Alfred A. Knopf, Inc., 1987.

Farmer, Fannie. *Boston Cooking-School Cookbook*. Boston: Little, Brown & Company, 1918; revised edition, 1930.

———. *Catering for Special Occasions*. Philadelphia: D. McKay, 1911.

Food and Drink: A Pictorial Archive from 19th-Century Sources, 3rd ed. Selected by Jim Harter. New York: Dover Publications, Inc., 1979.

Fowler, Damon Lee. *Classical Southern Cooking*. New York: Crown Publishers, Inc., 1995.

Garrison, Holly. *The Thanksgiving Cookbook*. New York: Macmillan Publishers, 1991.

Gerard, John. *The Herbal or General History of Plants*, 1633. New York: Dover, 1975 (reprint).

Gildrie, Richard P. "The Ceremonial Puritan Days of Humiliation and Thanksgiving," *The New England Quarterly*, 136:3-16. January 1982.

Gookin, Daniel. *Historical Collections of the Indians in New England*, 1674. New York: Arno Press, 1975 (reprint).

Hale, Sarah Josepha Buell. *The Good Housekeeper: Or, The Way to Live Well and to Be Well While We Live*. Boston: Weeks, Jordan, 1839.

Harland, Marian. *Dinner Year-Book*. New York: Scribner's, 1878.

Harrison, William. *The Description of England* (1587). Edited by Georges Edelen. London: Folger Library, 1994.

Heal, Felicity. *Hospitality in Early Modern England*. Oxford: Clarendon Press, 1990.

Heath, Dwight B., ed. *A Journal of the Pilgrims at Plymouth (Mourt's Relation)*. New York: Corinth Books, 1963. Cambridge: Applewood Books, 1986 (reprint).

Henderson, Mary. *Practical Cooking and Dinner Giving*. New York, London: Harper & Brothers, 1904.

Hibben, Sheila. *American Regional Cookery*. Boston: Little, Brown & Company, 1946.

———. *The National Cookbook*. New York: Harper & Brothers Publishers, 1932.

Hom, Ken. *Easy Family Recipes from a Chinese American Childhood*. New York: Knopf, 1997.

Howland, Mrs. E. A. *The New England Economical Housekeeper*. Worcester, Mass.: S. A. Howland, 1845.

Hutton, Ronald. *Stations of the Sun: A History of the Ritual Year in Britain*. Oxford: Oxford University Press, 1996.

———. "The Making of the Domestic Occasion: The History of Thanksgiving in the United States," *Journal of Social History*, 32(4): 373-389. Summer 1999.

Jacoby, Tamar, ed. *Reinventing the Melting Pot: The New Immigrants and What It Means to Be American*. New York: Basic Books, 2004.

James, Sydney V., ed. *Three Visitors to Early Plymouth*. Plymouth: Plimoth Plantation, 1963.

Johnson, Edward. *Wonder Working Providence*, 1654.

Josselyn, John. *John Josselyn, Colonial Traveler.* Edited by Paul J. Lindholdt. Hanover, N.H., and London: University Press of New England, 1988.

———. *New-Englands Rarities Discovered,* 1672. Boston: Massachusetts Historical Society, 1975 (reprint).

Lauden, Rachel. *The Food of Paradise: Exploring Hawaii's Culinary Heritage.* Honolulu: University of Hawai'i Press, 1996.

Lea, Elizabeth Ellicott. *Domestic Cookery, Useful Receipts, and Hints to Young Housekeepers,* 1853.

Leslie, Eliza. *New Receipts for Cooking,* 1854.

Love, William DeLoss. *The Fast and Thanksgiving Days of New England.* Boston: Houghton, Mifflin, 1895.

Lovegren, Sylvia. *Fashionable Foods: Seven Decades of Food Fads.* New York: Macmillan, 1996.

Many Thanksgivings: Teaching Thanksgiving—Including the Wampanoag Perspective. Boston: The Children's Museum, 2002

Mariani, John. *The Dictionary of American Food and Drink.* New Haven, Conn.: Ticknor and Fields, 1983.

Markham, Gervase. *The English Huswife,* 1615. Edited by Michael Best. Kingston, Ont.: McGill–Queen's University Press, 1986 (reprint).

McGee, Harold. *On Food and Cooking.* New York: Simon & Schuster, 1997.

Moosewood Collective. *Moosewood Restaurant Daily Special.* New York: Clarkson N. Potter, 1999.

Morton, Thomas. *New English Canaan or New Canaan,* 1637. New York: Burt Franklin, 1967 (reprint).

Murrell, John. *A Booke of Cookerie,* 1621.

———. *A New Booke of Cookerie,* 1615. Amsterdam: Theatrum Orbis Terrarum, 1972 (reprint).

Oliver, Sandra L. *Saltwater Foodways: New Englanders and Their Food, at Sea and Ashore in the Nineteenth Century.* Mystic, Conn.: Mystic Seaport Museum, 1995.

O'Neil, Molly. *New York Cook Book.* New York: Workman Publishing, 1992.

O'Neill Grace, Catherine, and Margaret M. Bruchae with Plimoth Plantation. Photographs by Sisse Brimberg and Cotton Coulson. *1621: A New Look at Thanksgiving.* Washington: National Geographic, 2001.

Paddleford, Clementine. *How America Eats.* New York: Scribner, 1960.

Parkinson, John. *Paradisi in Sole, Paradisus Terrestris,* 1629. Reprinted as *A Garden of Pleasant Flowers.* New York: Dover, 1976.

Parloa, Maria. *The Appledore Cookbook.* Boston: Andrew F. Graves, 1880.

Pleck, Elizabeth H. *Celebrating the Family: Ethnicity, Consumer Culture and Family Rituals.* Cambridge: Harvard University Press, 2000.

Rombauer, Irma. *The Joy of Cooking.* New York: Scribner, 1931, 1936 (second revision)

Rombauer, Irma, and Marion Rombauer Becker. *The Joy of Cooking.* New York: Scribner, 1951 (third revision), 1962 (fourth revision), 1975 (fifth revision), 1997 (sixth revision).

Root, Grace Cogswell. *Father and Daughter: A Collection of Cogswell Family Letters and Diaries, 1772–1830.* West Hartford, Conn.: American School for the Deaf, 1924.

Russell, William S. *Guide to Plymouth and Recollections of the Pilgrims Boston.* George Coolidge, 1846.

Seale, Doris. *Thanksgiving: A Native Perspective.* Berkeley, Calif.: Oyate, 1996.

Shapiro, Laura. *Perfection Salad.* New York: Modern Library, 2001.

———. *Something from the Oven.* New York: Viking Books, 2004.

Simmons, Amelia. *American Cookery.* Hartford, Conn.: Hudson & Goodwin, 1796.

Siskind, Janet. "The Invention of Thanksgiving: A Ritual of American Nationality," *Critique of Anthropology,* 12(2): 167-191. 1992.

Smith, John. *A General History of Virginia.* London, 1624.

Stowe, Harriet Beecher. *Oldtown Folks.* Boston: Houghton, Mifflin, and Company, 1891.

Wakefield, Ruth. *Ruth Wakefield's Toll House Tried and True Recipes,* 1945.

Wheeler, Grace Denison. *Grace Wheeler's Memories.* Stonington, Conn.: Pequot Press, 1948.

Williams, Susan. *Savory Suppers and Fashionable Feasts: Dining in Victorian America.* Knoxville: University of Tennessee Press, 1996.

Winship, George P. *Sailors' Narratives of Voyages along the New England Coast, 1524–1624.* Boston: Houghton Mifflin, 1905.

Winslow, Edward. "A Letter Sent from New England," in *A Relation or Journal of the English Plantation Settled at Plymouth in New England,* 1622. Edited by Dwight B. Heath as *Mourt's Relation.* New York: Corinth Books, 1963.

Winthrop, John, Jr. "Indian Corn," 1662, in "John Winthrop, Jr. on Indian Corn," by Fulmer Mood. *The New England Quarterly* 10, March 1927.

Wood, William. *New England's Prospect,* 1634. Edited by Alden T. Vaughn. Amherst: University of Massachusetts Press, 1977 (reprint).

www.eatturkey.com. The National Turkey Federation website.

www.jellomuseum.com. LeRoy Historical Society website.

www.karosyrup.com. Karo Syrup website.

www.oceanspray.com. Ocean Spray Cranberries website.

www.pilgrimhall.org. Pilgrim Hall Museum website.

www.verybestbaking.com. Libby's website.

Wyman, Carolyn. *Jell-O: A Biography.* Harvest Books, 2001.

Young, Alexander, ed. *Chronicles of the Pilgrim Fathers,* 1844. Baltimore: Genealogical Publishing Co., 1974 (reprint).

Credits

Index